CW00321995

A NEW WINDMILL COLLECTION
OF DIFFERENT TEXT TYPES

PERFECT MATCH

EDITED BY
MIKE GOULD

www.heinemann.co.uk
✓ Free online support
✓ Useful weblinks
✓ 24 hour online ordering

01865 888058

Heinemann Educational Publishers
Halley Court, Jordan Hill, Oxford OX2 8EJ
Part of Harcourt Education

Heinemann is the registered trademark of Harcourt Education Limited

Selection, introductions and activities © Mike Gould, 2004

First published 2004

09 08 07 06 05 04
10 9 8 7 6 5 4 3 2 1

British Library Cataloguing in Publication Data is available
from the British Library on request.

ISBN 0 435 13087 0

Express code: 0870P

Photos: p1 Rex Features/Mark Pain; p4 Topham Picturepoint;
p12 Empics; p33 Topham Picturepoint/Empics; p75 Topham Picturepoint/
Prosport; p127 Rex Features/ISOPRESS; p132 Rex Features/Jason Mitchell;
p144 Action Plus/Tom Hauck; p153 Topham Picturepoint/Empics

Cover design by Forepoint
Cover photo: © Imagestate

Typeset by ✏ Tek-Art, Croydon, Surrey

Printed and bound in the United Kingdom by Clays Ltd, St Ives plc

This book is for my son Sam, who plays and knows the game better than I ever did; for Bexhill Town Under 13s; and for Eric Cantona, who rescued my team from twenty-six years of hurt.

Prologue

'His face told me everything I needed to know. His rage. His frustration. I was sure I was finished.'

David Beckham

'It is not an offence in itself to be in an offside position.'

Extract from the Offside Rule (Law Eleven)

'I've been hurt, but from Oldham to Chelsea, from Liverpool to Luton, my heart beats to the rhythm of the fans.'

Eric Cantona

'Later that night, when the children were in bed, I went back to the Games Room and sat in a plastic chair and stared at the football table. The herd of men was still and silent. Each row was at an odd angle, some tipped forwards, some backwards.

I think: this is what rigor mortis would look like, if two teams were to die on the pitch and be skewered on long pins. Human kebabs.'

Liz Jensen (from the story 'Sent off')

'As soon as I came off the pitch I forgot about it. There's more to life than football.'

David Batty (on failing to score a penalty against Argentina in the 1998 World Cup)

Contents

Introduction for teachers

This collection has a dual purpose. First, and most importantly, it provides a range of texts separated into broad categories designed to address key areas of the Framework for teaching English. Secondly, by focusing on the subject of football, in all its manifestations, it is designed to motivate and stimulate those who might perhaps be less inclined towards other subjects and topic areas.

It was vital for me that the texts included should be of high quality, even if that quality is sometimes defined by the needs of the audience: clearly, a magazine spread extolling the virtues of Ruud van Nistelrooy does not require the same techniques as a more serious investigation about the future for Iraq's footballers. In addition, the texts selected range from populist and accessible, like the *Dream Team* script, to ones that are especially suitable for higher attainers, such as 'Corner flags and corner shops'.

Activities are provided for each extract in the book, although there is no suggestion that teachers complete every extract and every activity – that will depend on time and the focus of the scheme of work. Each set of individual activities also concludes with work on comparing texts within the section.

The activities themselves range between focused work at Word and Sentence level to an overview of the text as a whole. The framework objectives grid at the end of the book provides cross-references to specific objectives, should they be needed, but essentially the collection has been designed to be very flexible. Differentiation is provided through activities which start with questions focused on the text, moving towards more open, extended questions at the end. The latter tasks may require a greater degree of guidance and support.

Online assistance is provided for one particular activity. 'Watching the treble' requires students to translate football terminology into 'English'. A glossary list with answers will help you mark this activity, in case football is not your first love! For your convenience, a football glossary list for the whole book is also included on the Heinemann website.

Finally, this is not a book produced solely with boys – or indeed football fanatics – in mind. As well as female perspectives on the game, there are texts about hating football, and about the things that are wrong at the heart of the game. The game – good or bad – is like great drama, with all the same ingredients: heroes, villains, plots and sub-plots, and off-stage action.

In the end, good writing is good writing – whatever the subject – and if these texts can provide models for students' own writing then this book has succeeded. I hope you and your students find the texts enjoyable to read and study; it may not be as good as playing the game – but it certainly comes close!

Mike Gould

Introduction for students

Whether you love it or hate it – or don't really care one way or the other – one thing is for certain: football plays a central part in life today. Our newspapers and magazines are full of football celebrities; important matches draw millions of viewers from across the world; fashions and brands are built around football clubs and their players; and issues that happen in or around football reflect issues in society at large – like racism or hooliganism.

The writers in this book write about football for all sorts of reasons, because – like you – they love it, hate it or don't really care that much about it. In writing about football they are able to explore lots of ideas and write in a wide range of styles.

Sometimes, as in the article, 'In Iraq, young players dream of Premiership glory', the writer wants to show us another side to an issue, in this case the effects of the war in Iraq. In others, such as 'An evening with Gary Lineker', the aim is to make us laugh, to entertain us.

It is easy to think that writing about football is mostly concerned with reporting matches. As I hope you will see from this collection, it is about a great deal more.

Mike Gould

Section 1
Players and watchers:
Autobiography and Biography

An autobiography is a piece of writing by someone about his or her own life; a biography is someone's life-story written by someone else. People involved with football, whether managers, players, wives, children, or agents, are the ideal subject matter for these types of text. After all, many are in the public eye, and if they wish to tell the 'real story' of their lives, what better way than to tell it in their own words, or allow someone else to tell it for them. This section deals with such texts – not just the traditional ones you see on the shelves of bookshops, but also those from websites and newspaper profiles, which can also be forms of biography in their own way.

The Munich air crash
Sir Matt Busby

Football autobiographies are commonplace now, but once they were quite rare. In this example, Sir Matt Busby, then manager of Manchester United, recalls an event that affected everyone, even non-football fans. In 1958 the vast majority of his team were killed or injured in a plane crash in Munich, Germany. It was especially shocking as the team, known as the 'Busby Babes', had an average age of 21 and were already champions of Division 1(then the top league).

I have tried to collect my thoughts, my recollections of the whole nightmare from those moments waiting in Munich Airport. Here they are:

People who fly many journeys know the sounds. The drone of the Elizabethan's engines exploded into a roar and the big aircraft charged along the runway. Nothing unusual about this. Some people, whose courage in face of any other calls upon it would never fail them, will not fly in aeroplanes at all.

Those who *do* fly in them, often, will know that this first moment, when the engine's drone becomes a crack of thunder announcing take-off time, gives a little twist to the most hardened stomach, a twist of tension, a feeling of, 'This is it, God help us.' Men will hide their fears, since no man likes to look 'chicken', but those fears are there all right, until, **paradoxically**, the aircraft is up in the 'safety' of the air.

But we did not take off. The roar returned to a drone, we turned round, and idled back along the runway.

---

paradoxically: in a way that seems to contradict the situation

If take-off brings on that twinge of tension, take-off failure does nothing to reduce it. But the time came when we roared along that runway again. And again the roar stopped, and we droned and turned again and idled back. Two take-off failures were alarming.

Had we been in a depressed state after defeat we might have been more **apprehensive**. As it was we had just won our way into the semi-final of the European Cup, a most cheerful situation.

We settled back yet again, and again we sped in a great din of engines. But we sped on and on and on and my thoughts sounded just like that – 'On and on and on and on' – until they changed to 'Too long, too long, too long, too long!' We were not going up.

My next glimpse in the mists of memory is of throwing out my arms in a pathetic attempt at self-protection, and then of the world crashing in on us.

Next I see through those mists a brief, a fleeting glance in a snatch of consciousness. I see a big room with several covered bodies in it. I think I can hear now a doctor looking down at one of them and saying: 'This one is dead.' I have always had a feeling it was **Frank Swift**, I don't know why. Then I heard **Professor Maurer** telling the doctor to keep quiet.

Jimmy McGuire, President of the United States Football Association, arrived in Munich next morning. I was very ill, but not too ill to recognise my dear old friend. He spoke to me. I nodded. It was enough.

I know now that little hope was held for me. The Professor banished everybody from my bedside. He did

---

apprehensive: worried, anxious
Frank Swift: hugely popular goalkeeper in the1930s and 1940s, who became a sportswriter for the *Daily Mail* and died in the Munich air disaster
Professor Maurer: chief surgeon at the hospital

not want anything to knock me back. All I could feel, all I knew about at that time, was the pain. Then day after day, instinctively, gradually I began to feel that something terrible had happened. But it was not until about two weeks after the crash that I overheard a **clergyman** saying: 'Duncan Edwards is dead.' And then, for the first time, it really dawned on me. I really knew, though I had no idea what, that something even more terrible than I could imagine had struck, and that they were keeping it from me.

My wife, Jean, was at my bedside. When I asked what had happened she changed the subject. 'Don't worry,' she would say. 'Don't talk. I'm supposed to do the talking.'

Finally I could stand it no longer. I said: 'Jean, I want to know. I want to know the worst. For my peace of mind.' So began a new torture, for Jean and for me. I would name a name and without saying a word she would nod or shake her head. When even now I think about her

---

clergyman: someone who works for the Church

feelings at that time, let alone mine, in those dreadful moments of telling me about those poor kids, and those other lost friends, I could weep, and I am not by nature a weeping man.

This new torture, this constant mental torture, knocked me back and I was as near the brink as ever.

I was spared, but even if I survived how could I face the loved ones of the lads who were not spared? 'Was I to blame? Was I to blame? Why can't I die?'

The physical agony remained without let-up. Coughing was painful even to think about. When coughing, as I inevitably did, the pain was so **excruciating** that an old ward sister used to lean over me and I pulled most fearful faces and when it was over she would say: 'Wunderbar, Mr Boosby.'

Lung punctures, broken-bone manipulation, torn-flesh repairs without anaesthetics were a regular drill of **undiminishing** horror.

But even when I had talked myself out of my self-condemnation and self-blame on those two counts, my mental state was worse than the physical pain. 'I will never go back into football,' I would say, and this went on for weeks. But Jean, in her wisdom again, said: 'I don't think you are being fair to the people who have lost their loved ones. And I am sure those who have gone, too, would have wanted you to carry on.'

This plea went straight to the **crux** of the real matter. Jean's wisdom, commonsense and logic won. And had I not some more foster sons to look after? I must not let them down. Or their parents.

From that moment I wanted to live.

---

excruciating: terribly painful
undiminishing: never getting less
crux: central or most important part

Don't call her Ronaldinha
Anjana Gadgil

Being the wife or girlfriend of a football player can be a burden at the best of times. But what about when you are the wife of the player many consider to be the best in the world at that time? In this interview, taken from a BBC sports website, Milene Domingues reveals how she is quite a footballer in her own right.

Don't call her Ronaldinha

Milene Domingues has a problem. She has played club football since the age of 14, and holds the world record for **keepie-uppies** (55,187 touches in nine hours and six minutes). She broke the European transfer fee record when the Spanish club Rayo Vallecano tried to sign her, and is now the most recognisable female footballer playing on this side of the Atlantic.

Yet still everyone persists in calling her Mrs Ronaldo, or Ronaldinha, after her husband of three years and World Footballer of the Year, Ronaldo.

'I have my own name,' the 23-year-old says, grimacing. 'And all Ronaldo's girlfriends have been nicknamed Ronaldinha.'

But this is the one time during our interview that Milene looks unhappy. She

---

keepie-uppies: informal term for 'keeping the ball in the air'

has a wide smile on her face and chats away **disarmingly**, oblivious to the photographer's attentions, as you would expect from someone who has seen themselves plastered up on billboards since the age of 17.

So how did the girl from the suburbs of Sao Paolo in Brazil find herself the target of all this media attention? It all began with three brothers and a back yard.

'I always played football with my brothers in Brazil,' the 23-year-old grins. 'I never went anywhere without a football, I was like a tomboy.'

What did her parents and her peers think of her obsession? 'They preferred that I didn't play football. Everyone said that I could be a model so my mother took me along to an agency.'

Whenever she was at the agency, she would practise keepie-uppies during her breaks. And it was then that she was spotted, not for her looks, but for her ability with the ball.

'The director of the agency saw me and asked me to show him what I could do. So I did 100 keepie-uppies. He was impressed and told me to go to Corinthians where he knew the director. My mum wouldn't let me go, but I went anyway.'

As well as playing for the women's team, she was invited to entertain the crowd at half-time with her ball-juggling skills, for which she was paid enough money to appease her mother.

When she was 17, it was decided she would attempt the ball-juggling world record. Planned **meticulously**, Milene had to learn how to eat and urinate with the ball balanced on the back of her

---

disarmingly: in a way that gains someone's trust
meticulously: with extreme care and detail

head. Nine hours and six minutes later she was a Brazilian sensation, *rainha das embaixadinhas* – the juggling queen. So when she married Ronaldo at 20, she was hardly fazed by the media hype.

The same year they married, she gave birth to Ronald and moved to Milan, where Ronaldo was playing for Internazionale. However, when Ronaldo made his controversial move away from Milan to Real Madrid last summer, Milene didn't want to go.

'I have lots of friends in Milan, footballing and non-footballing, and none in Madrid.'

After three years away from football to bring up Ronald, Milene reckoned at least she could join a Spanish team. Many top clubs came for her signature on the basis of her reputation, but it was only after she was offered a contract worth well over £100,000 a year by Rayo Vallecano, the smaller of Madrid's three big clubs,

that the flaw became apparent.

'They were not allowed to have foreign women playing competitively for them. I could only train.'

So Milene took the unusual step of commuting back to Milan every weekend to play for the club she used to train with, Fiamma Monza, currently third in the Women's Serie A. But she believes that the effort is worth it.

'Travelling to and fro is tiring, but it's my passion. You can only play football when you are young, and I want to play as much as I can. It's my passion.'

However, she won't be travelling to China with the Brazilian national team this summer to compete in the World Cup.

'I don't want to be at that position when I have to leave my family for a long period to go and play football. I'm happy playing at the level I am.'

Then laughing, Milene adds, 'Also, I haven't been selected!'

Footballers' wives tell their tales
Shelley Webb and Kirsty Dailly

In this extract, Kirsty Dailly, wife of Scottish international player Christian Dailly, describes how she met her husband, and Christian's experiences at his first soccer club, Dundee United. In it, she reveals how home life can sometimes get in the way of professional football – especially when children come along.

Christian and I met at school. He was a year older than me and in my brother's class. You know what it's like in the playground and Christian was one of those really popular guys – he was the centre of attention, always laughing and having a good time. He'd be playing football in the playground and he was always one of the best. The girls all used to watch out for him in the corridors: 'Oh, look, there's Christian Dailly.' We went out when I was 14. Christian was my first ever boyfriend, but I chucked him after six weeks. I can't remember why exactly.

Christian left school at 16 and soon began playing in Dundee United's first team but he appeared at the school one day and walked me home. He then phoned and we went out again. I got a bit of stick from my friends who said, you're only going out with him because he's a footballer. But it wasn't that at all. I hadn't seen him for a long time and you know when you're with somebody and you feel comfortable and since then, since I was 15, we've always been together.

I left school at 17 and this was when I went to France to study French, geography and literature. Christian and I missed each other horrendously, but the experience was well worth the year apart. I still have a big box of letters that he sent. He was very good. I received at least one a

week but of course his box of letters from me is bigger –
I think I started off writing eight a week. While I was
there, I applied to do a hotel and catering management
degree and took up an offer from Edinburgh University.
So Christian and I had another year apart, although
I became pregnant with Rosie so that was the end of
my degree.

By the time Rosie was due, Dundee United were in the
middle of the build-up for their Coca-Cola Cup semi-final
match against Celtic. She eventually arrived on Monday
morning and Christian phoned in to the club to say he
was missing training that day to be at the birth. As the
semi-final wasn't until the Wednesday night he didn't
think there would be a problem and rang the club to say
he'd meet them in Glasgow. But no, this wasn't good
enough and the message from the manager Ivan Golac,
was: 'Stay there, Christian, just don't bother coming.
You're not in the squad – you're dropped.'

Apparently he'd got his priorities all wrong wanting
to be with me at the birth of his first child. Heaven
forbid. The press had a field day. We were bombarded at
the hospital by phone calls. A TV crew was waiting on the
doorstep when Christian got home. We were under siege
and all I kept thinking was, *this is strange. What's the
interest? I've just had a baby*. I was only 19 and I wasn't
used to press attention. It was scary and unwelcome.
They wanted photographs but nobody looks their best
when they've just had a baby so there was no chance of
that. But of course they didn't want a nice photograph so
they could say congratulations to Kirsty and Christian on
the birth of your first daughter. They wanted it to show
the reason why Golac dropped Dailly. Footballers have
got to get used to press attention but this wasn't fair, and
it wasn't fair of the manager. He knew exactly what he was
doing. He used the papers over the next couple of days
to say he had been misunderstood. Apparently he hadn't

dropped Christian because he missed training but because he would not be in the right frame of mind. Sure.

By contrast, at Derby County, when our second daughter Christy was born the day before Derby played Arsenal, Christian also missed training but still played the next day and in fact won the Man of the Match award.

I think our treatment at Dundee United may have had something to do with the fact that Christian had been there such a long time. Thirteen years. He'd played for them since he was a little boy and the footballing education he received there was second to none, but until we left he was still seen as a boy.

The first Indian footballer
Michael Lee

In this extract from a web article, Bhaichung Bhutia, captain of the Indian national soccer team at the time of writing, describes the difficulties of trying to succeed in the home of football. He also talks about the contrast between the life he leads in the UK, and the one he left behind in Bengal.

Bhaichung 'Chip' Bhutia is the captain of the Indian national team. Aged 25, he joined the Second Division English club Bury in September 1999 on a free transfer after trials with Aston Villa. As the first Indian player ever to play in the English football league, Bhutia has attracted a great deal of attention both in England, and back home, where Bhutia was accustomed to playing in front of

crowds of up to 140,000 in East Bengal's Salt Lake stadium.

As Bhutia recalls, it was some contrast coming to Bury, whose average gates are around 3000! He even admits, 'I'd never heard of Bury, and they weren't even in the picture when I came over from India to trial with some English clubs. My agent spoke to somebody who knew Bury's manager at that time, Neil Warnock, and a trial was arranged for me. I did very well, scored a couple of good goals and eventually signed a three-year contract.'

The first few months were a huge learning process for Bhaichung as he struggled to adapt to the physical nature of Second Division football. But his willingness to respond positively to the challenge before him impressed the coaching staff at Bury.

Kevin Blackwell, then assistant manager at Bury, recalls that Bhutia worked extremely hard to improve his fitness levels. 'Despite being a hero in India, he was very willing to learn and would do the work when he had to. The game over here is ten times more physical than in India and he had to adjust to it. We knew that we would have to invest at least six to eight months in him before he would be up to speed. But he never moaned despite the hard work.'

Bhutia gradually began to force his way into the first team and was an immediate hit with the Bury fans. 'The fans definitely took to him . . . he loves to take players on and score goals and fans like that,' said Blackwell.

Bhutia scored his first goal against Chesterfield in April 2000 in a 1–1 draw, 'I can't really describe how it felt, but I was so delighted,' he said.

Unfortunately, Bhutia suffered a series of injuries in the following season, which severely limited his first team appearances. Bhutia has just returned from India following the end of their World Cup qualifying campaign in an extremely positive mood.

'I'm settling back in to life in England again,' he said.

'I've moved to a different house and feeling really good about things. I just hope this season can be much better than the last.'

Kevin Blackwell believes that Bhutia has already accomplished one significant achievement, 'As the first Indian to play in the English football league I hope that Bury have sent a message out to the Asian community in this country. There must be some great talent around and we hope we inspire some of them by showing that if they are good enough we'll give them a chance.'

Watching the treble
Roy Keane

In this extract from his autobiography, Roy Keane describes the most important football match he had ever been involved in for Manchester United: the 1999 European Champions League Final against Bayern Munich. If United beat Munich, they would have won a unique treble (the other two trophies being the FA Cup and FA Premier League). The downside of the match was that Keane himself wasn't playing, as he had been ruled out, following two yellow cards in earlier matches.

Here he describes the match, and his own feelings as time was running out with United losing 0–1.

We'd played Bayern home and away in the league phase of the competition. Both games were drawn. They were a good side, but beatable. Bayern were never going to tear you apart as, say, Real Madrid or Barcelona might do. They'd be steady. Defend well, pass the ball around, be patient, wait for their opening. Effenberg in midfield was their main man, he dictated the pace they played at.

Six minutes into the game we gifted them a soft goal. Ronnie Johnsen fouled their big centre-forward, Jancker, and Mario Basler scored with a less than unstoppable free-kick. After that, nothing much happened. Neither side seemed capable of rising to the occasion. Of course, Bayern had the goal and were even more comfortable in their predetermined pattern of play. We had to chase the game, patiently, lest we were caught on the counter-attack. Twice in the second half they hit the woodwork. Curiously, these near misses acted as a spur to our players. This United team is never beaten. We know how to intensify the rhythm of a game. Pass the ball, move, support the player on the ball: fight to win it back if you lose it, the deeper in their half the better.

Slowly, I felt the game turn. Looking at the clock, there were just under fifteen minutes to go. The manager substituted Jesper and Andy Cole, throwing on Teddy and Ole. You couldn't choose two better subs. Teddy could drop deep and get on the ball. Ole was just about the best goalscorer in Europe. The tempo of the game was bound to change anyway. Would the Germans adapt to answer the subtly different questions now being posed?

The answer was no. Watching this, my head was wrecked. Bayern were hanging on. Their back four were no longer out behind the ball. Their midfield players were camped in their own half. 'They've gone,' I said to Jimmy Ryan. 'We've got them.' We desperately needed a break. If you keep doing the right things, you'll get your break in every game. But the Germans were riding their luck, strung out across the edge of their penalty area. For a team with their reputation Bayern Munich were by now a shambles, as bad as bad can be: they were actually 'bottling' it big time. They couldn't possibly win the Champions League playing like this. Or could they? For all the pressure around their goal, we never created a clear-cut chance.

Down on the touchline the fourth official held up his board: three minutes of added time. Another corner for us. Peter Schmeichel was sprinting forward. I'd never seen that particular tactic work! Amazingly, this time it did. Becks swung in a beautifully flighted cross, the ball was half cleared to Ryan on the edge of the box. He mis-hit his shot — straight to Teddy, who poked it past the German keeper.

The **Nou Camp** erupted. Even now I can't adequately describe the emotion I felt at that moment. Relief,

---

Nou Camp: name of the stadium in Barcelona where the match took place

certainly. Satisfaction, for I felt the lads deserved to stay alive just as the Germans had not deserved to win the trophy by default. Most of all, I was pleased for the manager. Not for the first or last time he'd played his substitution cards shrewdly.

There was still a minute to go when Bayern restarted the game. They had now completely lost it. We got the ball back immediately. Back from the dead, we were now unbelievably chasing the winner. Bayern conceded another corner. Becks curled it to the near post, Teddy got the flick on, and Ole guided the ball into the back of the net.

I doubt if we'll ever see three minutes of football like that again. In the end the Champions League of 1998/99 went to the team that wanted it most. Heart won the day. I had played in twelve of the thirteen European games, yet I never felt so drained as I did at the end of those ninety-three minutes in Barcelona. Even at the best of times I've never been one for overdoing the celebrations on the pitch after big games (I usually save myself for the bar). In the Nou Camp that night Paul and I were reluctant to respond when the manager urged us forward to receive our medals. Yes, we had played a part in the European campaign, but the night belonged to the guys who'd done the business against Bayern. Paul and I were in football limbo, examples of the stark truth that lies at the core of professional football: you play for your team, for your club, for the fans, but first and foremost for yourself. Football is a very selfish game. No matter how many people tell me I deserve that Champions League medal, I know I don't. In fact, you could argue that my indiscipline came very close to costing us the treble.

Corner flags and corner shops
Sanjiev Johal

For every Asian player who makes it as a footballer now, there were hundreds of footballers from Asian backgrounds in the past who didn't. One of these was Sanjiev Johal. But he was certainly passionate enough about playing! In this extract from his book he looks back to the 1970s and describes using his father's shop as a pitch, and the matches he played at school.

When I reached an age when football started to become more than just a game and increasingly a passion, I wanted to play it anywhere I could. If it was too cold or wet outside, then I would take my plastic 'flyaway' football and kick it around the shop. Our premises were shaped like a perfect pitch. There were shelves and clothing rails all around the walls with a large playing area in the middle. On one wall there was a large stand on which the loose textiles (used for Asian dress such as the **salwar kameez**) were displayed. This stand made for perfect goals into which I could score at will. Either one of my friends would come around to the shop and have a game, or my youngest sister Raj would stand in as a goalkeeper. My older sisters Susan and Bal would not allow themselves to indulge in such boyish activity, especially in full view of the passing trade. The shop-floor football action would only be interrupted by the sound of the bell above the front door, which signalled the arrival of a customer. The football would stop and my mum would come out from the rear living quarters, yell at us

salwar kameez: loose trousers and long-sleeved tunic often worn by Indian, Pakistani and Bangladeshi women

for playing with the ball in the shop and then proceed to serve the awaiting customers. This was strange business practice, but one that the local clientele became warmly accustomed to.

Whilst the shop space gave me the chance to nurture my **nascent** soccer skills, it was at Bristnall Hall High School that my peers and I replicated the recognised genius of players such as Zico, Platini and Maradona. We didn't want to be a **Dougan**, with his limp long hair and a sad droopy moustache; we wanted to be like Maradona and Zico, with tanned skin, silky skills and elusive coolness. Whatever else Derek Dougan may have been, he wasn't really cool, not in the way that Maradona or Zico were cool – they were more than football players; they were superstars.

By the early to mid-eighties, white pupils were not the sole masters of the school playing field. Access to the football pitch no longer involved putting oneself in grave physical danger. Instead, the Asian and black schoolboys assumed one patch of the field for themselves; there they played their own game with teams made up almost entirely of black and Asian players. Some white kids would join in with this group, usually those who were already within these ethnic groups on some social level, but non-blacks and non-Asians took part in a separate match. Early on in my time at this school, the white part of the pitch was much the larger, and was watched by most of the girls. However, as the decade wore on, the greater ethnic presence amongst the lower years began to **manifest** itself in the classroom and in the playground. By the time I was in my final year at secondary school, the Asian boys were the first on the playing field. They were the first to get the football out

---

nascent: in the process of being born, beginning to develop
Dougan: (Derek) Dougan – Wolves striker, well-known at the time
manifest: to show or make known

and first to organise a game. It was no longer the case that we had to wait for an invitation to play alongside our white peers, or fearfully start a kick-about in a small corner of the pitch. Now we had our own team, we had our own crowd of female admirers and, most importantly, we were appreciated as amongst the best footballers in the year.

It wasn't the case that we had extended our ethnic **ghetto** to incorporate the playing field, the field itself was a patch of grass where kids of all colours and creeds enjoyed the game of football. In fact, teams were organised around the very difference between white kids and non-white kids. Crudely put, when we played football at break-times and lunch-times, it wasn't fourth years against fifth years, nor Form 5E against Form 5L, but Blacks v Whites. It was as simple and clearly defined as that. If you had white skin, then you were on the Whites side, if you were anything else, if you were anything other than white, anything other than English, you became embraced by the black team. In truth, there were only two or three Afro-Caribbean players in the Blacks team. The Blacks were made up mostly of Asians. **Retrospectively**, there was a political statement being made here by the non-white footballers in the school. They were defining their **allegiance** to, and defining themselves by, the broad black struggle, and the more potent black power movement; they were expressing a **solidarity** that united non-white citizens in their shared struggle against **systematic oppression**, cultural

---

ghetto: place where one racial or social group is isolated
retrospectively: looking back to the past
allegiance: loyalty or commitment
solidarity: being together because of common interests or standards
systematic oppression: being kept down in a very thorough and organised way

ignorance and racial intolerance. Or maybe they were merely organising a group of young lads into two **easily discernible** teams for a decent game of footie. The latter may be somewhat nearer the mark, but politics is never completely disengaged from sport.

Due to the lack of in-depth ability amongst the Whites, the better white players refrained from regularly participating in this daily fixture for fear of humiliation; this, in turn, meant that the Whites were little competition for the dominating Blacks, who had a wealth of talent to call upon. The **apolitical** nature of this contest was highlighted when a few of us from the Blacks made free transfers over to the Whites. One of the players who 'went over to the other side', Harjinder Malka, was a talented player who played every game as an exhibition, not allowing any consideration of the score to distract him from his **Fancy-Dan** swaggering on the pitch. Another **defector** to the Whites was Peter Panayai. Peter (also known as Chippy because his dad owned a fish and chip shop) was of a Greek-Cypriot background, a detail which, allied with the non-whiteness of his appearance, made him eligible for the Blacks. The fact that he was the most gifted player in the school only served to reiterate the Blacks' dominance over the Whites.

The third member of this treacherous **triumvirate** was myself. Admittedly, I was not in the same class of a Panayai, but at the time of my switch to the Whites side, I was in the greatest footballing form of my entire life, a level of consistent performance that I have never

---

easily discernible: clearly seen
apolitical: nothing to do with politics
Fancy-Dan: an arch-enemy of *Spiderman* whose fast and dazzling footwork as a Judo master earned him his name
defector: someone who joins the 'enemy'
triumvirate: group of three

managed to reproduce. Panayai himself rated me as being in the top three players in the school at the time. During this period the three of us transformed the ailing, lifeless Whites team from obliging **whipping boys** into a force to be reckoned with.

---

whipping boys: people who are blamed or punished for the mistakes of others; scapegoats

Activities

The Munich air crash

1 Matt Busby is looking back as an older man at the events surrounding the crash. At the *actual* time, how long was it before he became fully aware of the terrible tragedy that had occurred?

2 Matt Busby moves between use of the *past* tense and the *present* tense in this extract in order to make comments on his thoughts now and at the time of the crash.

Copy and complete this table, adding two more examples of some phrases or sentences in the present tense or past tense. Highlight or underline the verbs. Then consider in what other way this flitting between one tense and another suits what he is describing (think about what happens to him).

Example	Past tense	Present tense
'People who **fly** many journeys **know** the sounds.'		✓
'. . . we **had just won** our way into the semi-final . . .'	✓	

3 At the time of the crash, Matt Busby felt that he could never go back into football again. Why do you think he felt like that? How did his wife persuade him to carry on?

4 Answer the questions below by further researching the Munich air crash. You will need to focus on the key words below (names, or powerful words, such as 'legend', to refine your search).

- Why was it considered *especially* tragic that Duncan Edwards died? You are looking for people's viewpoints, e.g. 'tragic'.
- What future England legend, a very young player at the time, survived the crash, and went on to become England's all-time top scorer?

Don't call her Ronaldinha

1 Who is Milene Domingues?

2 Why does she object so strongly to being called 'Ronaldinha'?

3 We find out quite a lot about Milene from this interview with her. Complete the bullet-point list below (up to ten points), summing up what we are told about her:

- comes from Sao Paolo
- 23 years old
- married to Brazilian footballer Ronaldo

4 Imagine that you have been asked to contribute to a magazine feature called 'Almost famous'. You are married to a world-famous sports personality (it does not have to be soccer), but unlike Milene, you are *not* famous in your own right. Describe a typical day with your husband/wife, including your reaction when admirers appear.

Before you write, decide:

- Are you the jealous type? Or can you laugh it off?
- How do you feel about your partner's ex-boyfriends or girlfriends?
- Do you like the media attention?
- How did you meet your famous partner?

You could start:

The shopping trip would have been just fine if it hadn't been for . . .

Footballers' wives tell their tales

1 Although this text appeared in a book, it is in fact taken from a series of interviews conducted by the book's author, Shelley Webb, herself the wife of a former player, Neil Webb. This is why there are moments when the style of the text seems quite conversational, and seems to address the reader/listener directly. For example:

'You know what it's like in the playground. . .'
'But, no, this wasn't good enough. . .'

Find at least two other examples in the text of similar conversational phrases or sentences.

2 An interview needs to be planned beforehand. Which of these might have been questions Shelley Webb asked Kirsty?

a How did you meet Christian?		Yes/No
b How do you spend the money your husband earns?		Yes/No
c How did you cope with the press attention when your baby was born?		Yes/No
d What are Christian's ambitions for the future?		Yes/No
e Which team do you support?		Yes/No

3 Now, make a note of five additional questions *you* would ask. Write down the purpose of each question (for example, to find out more about her feelings towards her husband's chosen profession).

The first Indian footballer

This article combines an interview with Bhaichung himself
with extra biographical details, and the views of other people
on Bhaichung.

1 Find an example of:

- a direct quotation from Bhaichung about coming to
  England
- a comment from another person about how Bhaichung
  worked when he first arrived.

2 Although this article is supportive of Bhaichung's attempts
to succeed in the Football League, it does not pretend that
things have been easy. In your own words, sum up the
problems that he has had to face.

3 Imagine you are a professional footballer, about to sign for
an Indian club. Copy and complete the spider diagram
below, putting down any problems you might face.

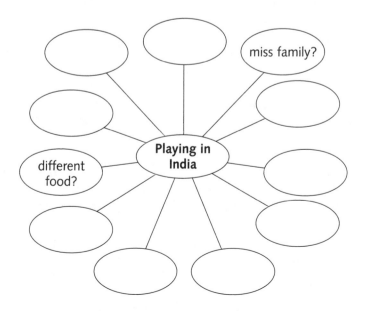

Watching the treble

1 This extract from Roy Keane's autobiography concentrates mostly on the events of the European Champions League final in 1999, and is therefore full of football-specific words and phrases that people unfamiliar with football might find difficult to understand.

Work in pairs (at least one of you should be a soccer fan who is familiar with football-specific words) and look at the phrases below. Find at least three other examples and create your own definitions, like the ones in the table.

Word/phrase	Meaning
'Bayern were **hanging on**'	The team called Bayern were only just able to prevent the other team scoring
'. . . Teddy, who **poked it** . . .'	Player called Teddy hit it with the toe of his boot (into the goal)
'. . . Teddy **got the flick on** . . .'	

2 Keane uses a number of techniques to convey the tension of the match. Find and write down at least one example of each technique listed below.

- References to the time passing in the game
- The use of questions to raise doubts and uncertainties
- References to his own feelings and emotions
- The use of short sentences in a paragraph to show the pace of the action.

3 For all the excitement and the emotion, what evidence is there that Roy Keane does *not* feel part of what happened by the end.

Corner flags and corner shops

This extract deals with one Asian boy's experiences of growing up playing football in the Midlands in the late 1970s and mid 1980s.

1 In which two places does Sanjiev develop his football skills?

2 Sanjiev contrasts a favourite Wolves player, Derek Dougan, with Maradona and Zico, by using expanded noun phrases. For example, Maradona and Zico are described as having 'tanned skin, silky skills and elusive coolness'. How is Dougan described?

> Remember, an expanded noun phrase means a noun that has had detail added to it. For example, 'the skilful boy' (noun phrase), 'with the cool trainers' (expanding the first description).

3 The second part of the extract deals mainly with the ethnic make-up of the school games, and most importantly, how things changed as the decade (the 1980s) developed. Find the relevant quotations within the text that match these points.

Point	Quotation/evidence
More pupils from an ethnic background joined the school.	
The girls liked watching the Asian players.	
Everybody, from whatever background, played football on the playing field.	
Teams were separated by their colour.	

4 Write your own brief description of school football, either as a spectator or a player. Try to include expanded noun phrases, and also some information on who is playing, and how the teams are organised (if you know!).

Write this in a similar style to the extract (that is, as a form of autobiography), giving some insights into school life.

Comparing texts

All the texts in this section deal, in one way or another, with the lives and experiences of players, their wives, managers or supporters. The following activities are designed to draw out the similarities and differences between the texts.

1 First of all, match up these simple descriptions of each text with the correct title.

1	Famous player recalls his team's greatest triumph	a	Don't call her Ronaldinha
2	Manager recalls tragic accident and fight for life	b	Corner flags and corner shops
3	Memories of school-days and school football	c	Footballers' wives tell their tales
4	Profile of first player from India to become professional in UK	d	The first Indian footballer
5	Scottish player's spouse recalls how they met	e	The Munich air crash
6	Famous player's wife asks to be taken seriously	f	Watching the treble

Now, write down your own alternative 'sub-headings' for each. For example, for **Don't call her Ronaldinha**, would 'Just a pretty face' work well as a sub-heading?

2 Only two of these texts deal with famous players/ managers recalling the past – the ones written by Roy Keane and Sir Matt Busby.

Look at both these texts again. What differences in style and choice of language do you notice between the two? For example, look at

- the *formality of language*. Roy Keane uses many football-specific terms. Does Sir Matt?
- the *chronology of events* – the order in which they took place. Does Roy Keane focus on one event in simple time order?

3 Both Milene Domingues and Kirsty Dailly are married to professional footballers, but there are as many differences between their lives as there are similarities. Use the writing frame below to write a comparison of the two texts.

Milene and Kirsty are both married to …
However, Milene is married to someone who is … whilst …
They have different experiences of fame, too. On the one hand, Milene has got used to the pressures because …
However, Kirsty …
Both of them have experienced difficulties in being married to professional players. For example, Milene had to make a choice about …
I believe that of the two, the one who seems to be coping best with her life is … because …

4 The two extracts, **The first Indian footballer** and **Corner flags and corner shops**, both deal with the experience of Asian people in relation to football. However, one is concerned with a boy who has grown up in the UK and will never make it as a professional player, whilst the other is about a young professional player, new to the game in the UK. Write a letter from Sanjiev to Bhaichung, explaining why it is important for a player from the Asian sub-continent to succeed in the UK. You could start the letter like this:

Dear Bhaichung I am delighted to see you making such a success of your career in the UK. This is really important because …

Section 2
Facts, stats and news:
Non-fiction

This section deals with the way football is reported and analysed. Much of the pleasure in following football is not just in watching the games, or reading about the players' lives and views, but in finding out information and the background to matches. There is a whole industry now dedicated to the analysis of matches, as well as the reporting of games and tournaments. Much of this reporting, however, also touches on areas unrelated to the actual matches – business, crowd trouble, fashions, and so on.

Football's history
Philip's Encyclopedia

This text, taken from a large encyclopedia, is designed to give a brief, factual account of the history of the game, how the game is played, and recent developments.

---

football, association (soccer) Arguably the most popular worldwide sport. It involves two teams of 11 players who attempt to force a round ball into their opponents' goal. It is played on a rectangular pitch of maximum size 120 x 90m (390 x 300ft), minimum 90 x 45m (300 x 150ft). The goals, two uprights surmounted by a crossbar, are 7.32 x 2.44m (8 x 24ft) wide. Only the goalkeeper may handle the ball, and then only in the penalty area of the goal he is defending. The other players may play the ball in any direction with any other part of the body, essentially it is kicked or headed. A game is played over two 45-minute periods and controlled by a referee. Modern football rules were formulated in 19th-century England, and the Football Association (FA) was founded in 1863. The FA Cup, established in 1872, is the world's oldest knockout football competition. The introduction of professionalism in 1885 led to the foundation (1888) of the Football League Championship. Football soon spread beyond Britain and, in 1904, *Fédération*

Phillip's Encyclopedia

Internationale de Football Association (FIFA) was
formed to control the sport at world level. Football has
been played at the Olympic Games since 1908. The first
of the four-yearly World Cup competitions was held in
1930. In Europe, the winners of each national league
annually compete for the European Champions Cup
(established 1955). Recent years have seen a significant
increase in commercial sponsorship and television
coverage. In 1992 the English FA changed the 'four-
divisions' structure of the Football League, primarily to
raise the commercial profile of leading clubs. This
structure consisted of a 'Premier' league of the top 20
clubs as a separate entity within the FA, and the First,
Second and Third Divisions of the Football League.

The business of football
Sports Business Group at Deloitte

These figures are taken from a press release from the consultants in the Sports Business Group at Deloitte and show spending for the 2001/2002 season. Such statistics are widely available and demonstrate the extent to which football really has become a business.

PREMIERSHIP STATISTICS

➤ Premiership clubs' total turnover – £1.132 billion.

➤ Premiership clubs' total pre-tax loss – £137 million.

➤ Average Premiership club turnover – £56.6 million.

➤ Premiership clubs' total wages and salaries grew by 26 per cent to £706 million.

➤ The average Premiership club has income more than four times that of a Division One counterpart.

➤ Promotion to the Premier League is worth about £34 million.

TRANSFER SPENDING

➤ Total spending on player transfers by English clubs hit £407 million in 2001/02, down slightly on the previous season's record of £423 million.

➤ But for the 2002/03 season the total is expected to be only £150 million, with only £20–25 million being spent in the January transfer window.

MOST PROFITABLE ENGLISH CLUBS

Club	Profit
Manchester United	£33.9 million
Newcastle United	£14.8 million
Liverpool	£14.5 million
Tottenham Hotspur	£9.2 million
Chelsea	£8.1 million

Football and royalty
Martin Chatterton

In this extract from his book, *The Utterly Nutty History of Footy*, Martin Chatterton takes a sideways look at the history of football, sometimes mixing fact with complete fiction. In this extract, he describes the long-term connection between kings and queens and football, and how the game wasn't always as popular as it is today.

FOOTBALL & ROYALTY

You may think that the connection between football and royalty is limited to shaking hands with the teams on Cup Final day, or with the fact that Prince Charles is a dead ringer for the FA Cup itself (see opposite), but you would be mistaken.

The FA Cup

Prince Charles

In fact, attending big games is only a fairly recent event, first happening in 1914, when George V presented the trophy to Burnley.

Before this, most royals tended to be firmly of the opinion that footie was A BAD THING, with the game being banned by King Edward II in 1314:

When football became increasingly popular, it had one side effect which annoyed many British monarchs, including Edward III and Henry IV: it began to interfere with archery practice.

Elizabeth I and James I also banned the game from London and the court, and it wasn't until Charles II watched a top-flight Italian Serie A game in Florence that a royal showed any positive interest in the sport. Of course, nothing has changed since then; Italian football was still dead good but *totally* boring after a while.

The wonder of Ruud

Manchester United's official magazine, United

Most everyday fans, though affected by their club's spending, are probably most interested in fairly basic statistics – how many goals their team and players score, and whether this is more than their opponents! But club magazines often fill their pages with statistics designed to show their players in a good light. In 2003 the editor of *United* magazine produced this article to illustrate how good their main striker, Ruud van Nistelrooy, was.

THE **VITAL** STATISTICS

When, where and how does Ruud score his goals? Can Ronaldo and the rest match up to his striking prowess? All your questions (and some you didn't even ask) answered . . .

WHEN, WHERE AND HOW?

Of the 12 goals Ruud has scored between 41–50 minutes, 9 came in the 2001/02 season. This season he has been most prolific in the 61–70 minute period, scoring 6. Ruud only gets more dangerous as the match progresses, scoring 22 goals in the last half-hour, compared to 12 in the opening 30 minutes.

All of Ruud's 47 Premiership/ European goals for United in open play have been scored with shots from inside the box and 64 per cent (excluding penalties!) with his right foot. As for penalties, he has missed just one. 10 of the 11 penalties he's scored were struck into the keeper's right-hand corner. Video analysis shows they often dive the right way, but the power and placement means they can't stop it.

SIMPLY RUUD!

So what can you expect from Ruud when you go to watch a
United game? Well, the statistics show that at least half his shots
will be on target and there's a 70 per cent chance he'll score.

APPEARANCES	80
Minutes played	6,544
GOAL ATTEMPTS	
Goals	58
Shots on target	124
Shots off target	91

GOAL AVERAGES	
Minutes-between-goals	113
Goals-to-shots %	27
Shooting accuracy %	58
Goals-per-game	0.7
PASSING	
Goal assists	12

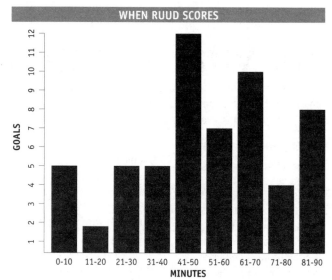

WHEN RUUD SCORES

WHERE		HOW		GROUND	
INSIDE*	47	RIGHT FOOT**	41	HOME	36
OUTSIDE*	0	LEFT FOOT	9	AWAY	22
PENALTIES	11	HEADERS	8	**TOTAL**	58

* in open play   ** includes penalties

RUUD v RONALDO & CO

Statistically, Ruud has been far and away the best striker in the group phases of this year's Champions League. He averages a goal every 50 minutes. Compare that to Internazionale's Christian Vieri, who has managed a single goal in 883 minutes and Ronaldo who waited 263 minutes between strikes. Only Filippo Inzaghi (41 per cent) of AC Milan and Internazionale's Hernan Crespo (35 per cent) come close to Ruud's incredible goals-to-shots ratio of 45 per cent. His clinical finishing contrasts sharply with Thierry Henry's hit-and-miss approach – whereas Ruud scored 10 goals from a mere 22 shots (18 on target, 4 off target), Henry's 7-goal tally came from 43 shots (21 on target, 22 off target).

RUUD VAN NISTELROOY v CHAMPIONS LEAGUE RIVALS 2002/03

*** Does not include qualifying matches	Ruud Van Nistelrooy	Hernan Crespo	Filippo Inzaghi	Thierry Henry	Raúl	Christian Vieri	Patrick Kluivert	Ronaldo
Appearances*	7	8	9	12	10	10	11	7
Minutes played	503	655	647	1,023	876	883	874	525
GOAL ATTEMPTS								
Goals	10	9	9	7	7	1	5	2
Shots on target	18	16	15	21	21	9	14	14
Shots off target	4	10	7	22	15	14	12	8
GOAL AVERAGES								
Minutes-between-goals	50	73	72	146	125	883	175	263
Goals-to shots %	45	35	41	16	19	4	19	9
Shooting accuracy %	82	62	68	49	58	39	54	64
Goals-per-game	1.4	1.1	1.0	0.6	0.7	0.1	0.5	0.3
PASSING								
Goal assists	3	1	0	3	5	1	1	3

Riot in Glasgow
The Scotsman

Facts and statistics are one thing; the news stories behind them another. In 1909, Celtic and Rangers played each other in a Scottish Cup Final replay. The facts state that the match, like the first, was drawn. However, most supporters amongst the 60,000 watching had been led to believe that if the match ended equal, an extra half-hour would be played. But, when the match ended, it soon became apparent that this wasn't the case, and the supporters on both sides – who wanted to see a result – rioted.

It would be impossible adequately to describe the many cruel incidents which went to make up a riot now proceeding in almost every quarter of the field. **Stricken** men fell with blood streaming from their wounds, and the rage and **tumult** became more intense. Many of the police were beaten and injured in the most brutal and **callous** fashion, and the force as a whole were the chief sufferers of the day. It was generally remarked that those of the crowd most active in the disturbance were composed of the most degraded section of the community, the self-respecting portion having as far as possible retired when the character of the **fray** became apparent. Thousands, however, who would gladly have quitted the scene, now found it impossible to leave, since those outside were massed at the exits, and outlet was a matter of great difficulty. Maddened by excitement, and relying on their

---

stricken: badly hurt
tumult: confusion and loud noise
callous: with no sympathy for other people
fray: fight or argument

overwhelming numbers, the rioters now proceeded to the extremest limits. The goalposts were attacked and uprooted, the nets torn to pieces, and the woodwork round the enclosure broken down to be used as weapons against the police. Acting with **commendable** patience and restraint, the police force, who were shortly reinforced by the arrival of reserves from almost every district in the city, persevered in their attempt to clear the ground. A number of mounted men were found to be of great assistance; but the mob took a **malicious** delight in surrounding the horsemen, and endeavouring to force them to dismount.

They beat man and horse most unmercifully, and in some cases the man was pulled to the ground. Not only had the police to persist in their own work of overcoming the mob, but they had to protect and rescue each other. Where a solitary policeman was trapped he was dealt with in the most outrageous manner, and it is little wonder that rumour had it that several of them had been killed.

The objective of the rioters, as has been indicated, was evidently the **dressing-boxes** of the players, but the police force was successful in repelling the attack. It was soon obvious, however, that new outlets for the prevalent passion had been found. Quantities of the broken barricading were collected, piled in a heap, and ignited. Quite a number of the crowd were in possession of bottles containing whisky, and they were actually seen to pour the fluid on the broken timber in order to aid its quicker ignition. Soon a huge bonfire was in progress, fed by fuel brought from every possible quarter. Attention was next directed to the pay boxes at the north-west entrance, and they were also soon a mass of flame. It was found necessary to summon the Fire Brigade, who arrived on the scene

---

commendable: praiseworthy, worthy of approval
malicious: with the intention of hurting
dressing-boxes: changing rooms

shortly after six o'clock. The defenceless firemen were on their arrival **maltreated** in similar fashion to the police, and at least one of them, John Kennedy, of the Queen's Park Division, was seriously injured. He is suffering from a number of broken ribs. When the firemen attempted to set to work their hose-pipes were seized and thrown into the flames. Others, which were brought into position, were cut and hacked at with knives. Stones, bottles, and the other available missiles were hurled at the firemen, who of course were quite unable to defend themselves. Ultimately they succeeded in extinguishing the fire, but not before very considerable damage was done.

When all the reserves had been hurried up from the district police offices, there would be about 200 constables on the field, including about sixteen horsemen. The difficulty was to drive the crowds up the slopes surrounding the pitch, and the method adopted was to force them out of the ground in batches. But long before comparative order had been restored, the casualty list had reached appalling proportions. A number of medical men who happened to be present set themselves devotedly to the work of attending to the injured. These gentlemen included two doctors, Jamieson, father and son, and Dr D. M'Ardle, of Stothill Hospital. Later they were reinforced by assistance from the Victoria **Infirmary**, which is situated in the neighbourhood. Ambulance waggons were summoned, and, after being temporarily attended to, the sufferers were conveyed to the Victoria Infirmary. One of the injured was attended at the Royal Infirmary, which is several miles distant. The spectacle presented in the football pavilion and neighbourhood, where the medical work was proceeding, resembled nothing so much as what one would picture occurring in the heat of a battle.

---

maltreated: treated badly
infirmary: hospital

The Hillsborough disaster: 14 years on

The Guardian

This article, taken from *The Guardian* of 15 April 2003, looks back fourteen years to the day when Liverpool and Nottingham Forest met in an FA Cup semi-final at Sheffield Wednesday's Hillsborough stadium, a day when 96 Liverpool fans died after police opened a gate to avoid overcrowding. The article reports the key facts as they are remembered, but also *how* the tragedy occurred, and its aftermath.

Today is the 14th anniversary of the Hillsborough disaster at Sheffield in which 96 people were crushed to death during the 1989 FA Cup semi-final between Liverpool and Nottingham Forest.

That day, the way English football was watched, presented and financed changed forever.

Hillsborough had hosted many semi-finals, including the 1988 semi-final, also between Liverpool and Forest. The match programme in 1989 showed a picture of a full Leppings Lane end with a paragraph that read: 'As you look around Hillsborough you will appreciate why it has been regarded for so long as the perfect venue for all kinds of important matches. It is a stadium that befits such occasions and the large crowds they attract.' A year on the story was very different.

The warnings were there from the beginning. Liverpool had a larger support than Nottingham Forest, yet they were allocated the smaller end of the ground. By 2.30 p.m. a bottleneck had developed. Three gates and seven turnstiles were available to accommodate upwards of

10,000 fans. Coaches that arrived late, having been delayed by road works, hindered the situation further.

Already there were many fans inside the ground; and many still trying to get in meant conditions in the paddock were getting desperate. People's movements were restricted due to the number of people already inside, never mind those still trying to get in.

The 96 people who died that day died because of gross incompetence by the South Yorkshire Police. In particular, Chief Superintendent David Duckenfield, who failed, perhaps through lack of experience (many blamed his inexperience of handling such big games), to realise what was going on. And who, by his own admission, 'froze' when faced with a decision that took the lives of so many.

If events of that day weren't horrific enough, the events were compounded by coverage of one of the largest football disasters in modern British history by the *Sun*. The *Sun*'s editor of the day, Kelvin McKenzie, informed the British public of what he described as 'The Truth'. Tales of fans stealing from the dead and abusing police who were trying to administer aid to the injured and dying. This, of course, was not 'the truth'.

The headlines caused uproar in the city of Liverpool and beyond. The newspaper was burned in protest outside newsagents across Merseyside. The headline still haunts Liverpudlians, the families of those who died and survivors. The boycott of the *Sun* is ongoing and figures released showed that circulation figures in the region have never recovered from the boycott.

To add to the pain, the BBC recently sold footage rights of Hillsborough: the intention being that the images were to be used to highlight the effects of football violence.

The pursuit of justice by the families is ongoing. Battling against the lies and injustice is a daily struggle for all of those involved.

Liverpool legend Bill Shankly is constantly quoted as saying: 'Football isn't a matter of life or death. It's far more important than that.' After reading the accounts of the victim's families, survivors and witnesses you realise how insignificant football really is.

Pupil excluded over Beckham crop

BBC News

In May 2000, newspapers and other media reported the story of how a schoolboy had been excluded from school for copying the haircut David Beckham had at the time. This news story shows the extent to which celebrities, such as top professional players, influence the styles and fashions of the young.

Pupil excluded over Beckham crop

A teenage football fan has been excluded from school for getting a David Beckham haircut. Gary Brunskill was sent home after he copied the Manchester United star and had his head shaved.

His mother Michelle is furious with the school, Ribblesdale High School Technology College in Clitheroe, Lancashire. But head teacher Glynne Ward argues that Gary 'excluded himself', as he was well aware of rules about dress code and appearance.

Gary, 15, who actually supports Blackburn Rovers, says he decided to have his hair shaved because he 'fancied a change' of hairstyle.

'Smart and stylish'

'I've always had long hair, to just above my ears. I thought the close crop suited Beckham and I think it suits me,' he said. 'I think it's stupid I was sent home. A hairstyle doesn't change you, and it's better than my last one anyway, which was dyed blond with an undercut, and was a bit curly. Lots of people my age look up to people like Beckham, and they're bound to copy him.'

Mrs Brunskill, 36, said: 'If Beckham has had it cut short you can guarantee there will be a lot of boys copying him. I think it looks very smart and stylish, and it is ridiculous to expel him. The first thing they do when you get into the Army is cut your hair – so how can the style be okay for the military and Manchester United, but not Gary's school? They are supposed to be educating the person, not their hair.'

But Ms Ward said Gary and others in his year group had already been warned about hairstyles, and called the teenager's decision to shave his head an 'act of defiance'. She said Gary and another boy, who had also copied David Beckham's hairstyle, had been sent home from school, but had been allowed to return a few days later when their hair had started to grow. 'Teenagers are fashion-conscious, schools are not,' she said.

'Totally bald'

'If they want to dye their hair or be bald, they can do it during the summer holiday, when they've got six weeks off school. It does detract from learning, as it becomes an issue, a focus, and it can cause problems. An educational institution is not about making fashion statements. Gary looked totally bald, and enough is enough. I do think that when you have got these extremes of hairstyle it can lead kids into problems, giving out the wrong messages about the type of person they are. Where do you draw the line? They've been told in no uncertain terms what is inappropriate. They've got to learn, otherwise you're opening the door to all sorts of things.'

Ms Ward said she wished that 'image-makers' such as Beckham, would 'give some thought to what they're doing'.

'Often they don't realise what a knock-on effect it has on a vulnerable teenager,' she said.

Ronaldo and the World Cup Final 2002

Alan Pattullo

The following newspaper report of the World Cup final between Brazil and Germany in 2002 is included in this section as it appears to be simply an account of the goals and events that shaped the match. But, when you read it you will see this is much more like the review of a great drama or film, or even a battle . . . with a heroic central figure – Ronaldo.

The sparkling jewel in Brazil's world crown
Germany 0
Brazil 2
Ronaldo (68, 79)

REJOICE. **Retribution**. Ronaldo. These are the three Rs which mattered most to Brazilians yesterday, although Rivaldo and Ronaldinho, those other two **samba musketeers**, also played rich parts on a night of nights. It was almost excessively romantic. After four years in which the sting of life has taken considerable toll, Ronaldo was able to cast off the horror of career-threatening injuries and finally draw a line under Paris 1998, and the seizure which **enervated** him to such an extent that he was a bystander in that final.

Yesterday he passed us with a heroic tread, scoring twice in a match-winning, a World Cup-winning

---

retribution: paying back
samba musketeers: Brazilian heroes
enervated: took strength away, weakened

performance. The **brace** assured him the Golden Shoe, awarded to the tournament's highest goalscorer, but such things seem almost frivolous concerns amid all the other loot plundered, chief among them being surely this **redemption** of which we talk and which Ronaldo has sought since first setting foot in the Far East.

He has often during this tournament complained of people forever wishing to speak of Paris. Now those who stop, or more likely mob, him in the street will wish only to talk of Yokohama, and the night he communed with Pele. The legend's name was evoked here, and not simply because of the striking masterclass just witnessed. Pele's record of World Cup goals for Brazil is one he now shares with Ronaldo, who has sourced his 12 goals from one fewer World Cup.

With Germany in disarray, and with further opportunities for goals a distinct possibility, Ronaldo was replaced, something you first thought cruel. On reflection, however, Luiz Felipe Scolari's decision makes perfect sense. It was a night for these twin legends to intertwine, and not for one to win out over the other. There was no more memorable a moment than Pele's clasping of Ronaldo on the podium, a meeting of such importance that you almost expected Japan's famously fragile **plates** to violently shake with the seismic significance of it all.

In the end, though, there were no earth tremors, no falling stars, and no other **phenomenon** save for the one we came here yearning to see. Ronaldo – baby face grin, assassin's eyes, and the raised arms which signify a job completed, a demon banished.

---

brace: a pair, two things of the same kind
redemption: the act or moment of winning something back
plates: the blocks that form the earth's crust, which, in Japan, cause many earthquakes
phenomenon: an unusual fact, event or person

There were other, so many other, sights to savour. In fact, you did not know where to look at the end, so **teeming** with strands of extraordinary tales was this. There was Cafu, rising like the figure of Christ overlooking the bay at Rio, holding aloft the World Cup, possibly the nearest anyone comes to experiencing what it must be like to hold the world in their hands. This was his third consecutive World Cup final, a **hat-trick** he shares with no one else.

As if this team cannot boast enough. There was Ronaldinho, those great Bambi eyes almost bursting amid the wonder of it all. Then the squad, the entire squad including physios, fitness instructors and possibly even bingo callers, positioned themselves in a circle of joy, linking hands as if about to end all this with a burst of 'Auld Lang Syne'. Indeed, **Burns** would have liked it here, would have thrilled at the rollicking nature of the game, would have loved the twin human contours of great joy and great grief, and would have cherished, certainly, those Brazilian ladies who had yet more reason to wriggle merrily in the stands, shirts knotted above bare midriffs.

Yet what of Germany, a Ronaldo away from being world champions themselves but now free to console themselves only with strange talk of 'vice-world champions'? This awkward title was being banded about by various announcers, wishing only sweetness and light upon everyone, but you imagine the Germans to be first to shake it off.

Oliver Kahn was not for being comforted. In many ways this fellow shaped this match as much as Ronaldo, though not with the distinction expected. Rather

---

teeming: present in large quantities
hat-trick: three in a row
Burns: Robert Burns, famous Scottish poet and composer of 'Auld Lang Syne' ('the good old times')

prematurely named winner of the Yashin prize for goalkeeping excellence during the tournament in the morning, it needed only one slip, one fumble, for the award to turn to dead leaves in his hands. And so it agonisingly proved. Having been provoked, fate turned on him.

For Kahn, who brought Germany to this point with these very same palms, you weep. Four years after Ronaldo's agonies in Paris and eight years further on from Roberto Baggio's penalty miss in Los Angeles, a World Cup final has been framed by another tale of personal torment.

The game was, if anything, more Germany's at the point when Kahn undid all his previous good work, spilling Rivaldo's shot into the path of Ronaldo. The look of horror as he registered what had been done and what was inevitably about to follow could be football's equivalent of **Munch's *Scream***.

'I am fully aware this is my one and only mistake,' he later said, in a slightly typical German manner. 'It was brutally punished.'

He had no chance with Ronaldo's second 12 minutes later, a sweet finish after good work down the right flank by Kleberson and a neat dummy by Rivaldo, but this did not matter, least of all him. The game had gone already, and so too had Kahn, who stood muttering violent reproaches to himself.

At the final whistle, the keeper ripped his gloves from his hands and then leant silently against a post for what seemed an age. The German players arrived in a crocodile-line, one by one seeking to console him. It wasn't to be borne. Even referee Pierluigi Collina went to him, and whispered in his ear.

Munch's *Scream*: *The Scream* is a vivid painting by Edvard Munch, a Norwegian painter

When finally Kahn tore himself from the **vigil**, he left his gloves where he had thrown them, as though they had betrayed him. They probably linger there now, along with the lucky penny, the *glückspfennig*, the German players have buried in the turf of one penalty box before each World Cup game, its reserves of fortunes clearly having been expended after a tournament in which Rudi Völler's German team had seemed so favoured.

Amid all these snapshots, one which holds its charge: as the players leave the park at half-time, they one by one acknowledge the presence of the World Cup, resting on a table by the tunnel entrance, with nervous sideways glances, as though it were forbidden treasure, a burning sun too bright to gaze upon. Only Ronaldo fixes it with a stare, one that speaks of unfinished business. An hour later closure had arrived, via a brilliance that would blind us all.

Attendance: 69,029

Germany: Kahn, Linke, Ramelow, Metzelder, Frings, Schneider, Jeremies (Asamoah 77), Hamann, Bode (Ziege 84), Neuville, Klose (Bierhoff 73). Subs not used: Baumann, Bohme, Butt, Jancker, Kehl, Lehmann, Rehmer, Ricken.

Brazil: Marcos, Edmilson, Lucio, Roque Junior, Cafu, Kleberson, Gilberto, Carlos, Ronaldinho (Juninho 85), Rivaldo, Ronaldo (Denilson 90). Subs not used: Belleti, Ceni, Dida, Edilson, Junior, Kaka, Luizao, Polga, Ricardinho, Vampeta.

Referee: Pierluigi Collina (Italy).

---

vigil: keeping watch over something, often at night, when everyone else is sleeping

Activities

Football's history

This is quite clearly an informative text from an encyclopedia, designed to help show anyone who doesn't know what football is, how you play it, and its basic history. Such texts are intended to provide succinct, clear summaries, and whilst most people know the basic purpose of the game – to put the ball between the posts – not everyone will know how the game started.

1 The text provides information in three main areas:

- the rules/purpose of the game
- the 'older' history of the game
- the recent history of the game.

Find one example of each of these elements in the text.

2 We tend to think of texts such as these are simply informative and factual. Can you find any examples of an opinion or view being expressed in any form?
(Clue: look at the beginning of the text, and the end, where there is reference to the formation of the Premier League.)

3 Find any other encyclopedia which has an entry for association football, and note down any similarities or differences between that entry and this one.

- **a** What has been included in one but not the other?
- **b** Is the structure the same (dealing with the rules/purpose etc first)?
- **c** Is there any evidence of a viewpoint or attitude to football?

4 Write your own encyclopedia entry for football, using *your own words* and ensuring you say something about how to play the game, its history and current situation. The style should be clear, formal and direct.

For example:
'The game is played on a pitch which measures . . .'

The business of football

These figures are taken from a press release from the Consultants in the Sports Business Group at Deloitte and provide a simple, but very interesting insight into the finances of football. The original press release was significantly more complex and detailed, but the newspapers selected information such as the statistics in the extract to make various points about the English game.

1 If you were writing an article to prove how important it is to gain promotion to the Premier League, what information from the statistics would you use?

2 The information on the most profitable of the top clubs is presented as a list of bullet points. Present the same information in at least two other ways, for example:

   • graphs
   • pie-charts
   • tables or grids.

3 Here is some further information about European clubs and countries:

   • England's 'matchday incomes' are almost three times those of other big leagues (i.e. Serie A)
   • Total income (approx.) of all clubs in the 'big leagues' in Europe was 7.1 billion euros in 2001/2002.
   • English Premiership takes the largest individual share of this income – 25 per cent of 80 per cent produced by the main leagues.
   • Revenue growth (i.e. the money coming in) grew in England to 1.7 billion euros (21 per cent growth); to 1 billion euros (19 per cent increase) in Germany (for the first time), but in Italy they were down 2 per cent and in France stayed the same.

                    (Source: Sports Business Group at Deloitte)

Write a brief explanatory article in which you describe how well English football is doing compared with its neighbours in Europe. And you could also compare this with how well the England football team is doing on the pitch!

Use linking words/phrases such as:

On the one hand,	Nevertheless,
However,	Despite this,
In contrast,	Having said that,

Football and royalty

1 Martin Chatterton's text appears to be both informative *and*
amusing. But how does he make the historical information
interesting and funny? Here are some of the techniques he
uses. Can you find examples of them in the text?

- chatty, informal language
- humorous drawings
- mix of the old and new.

2 You will see that it was forbidden to play football back in
the fourteenth century. Imagine you have been caught
playing football and have been arrested.

Write the scene in which the king's local official comes to
your house with 'evidence' of your crime. Write it in the
form of the script, as in the example below. Make it
humorous if you can. You could add some modern
references, but also use 'mock' old-fashioned English – see
the box below for some words and phrases you could use.

For example:

KING'S OFFICIAL: Ah, good afternoon **my good man**. Do I
have the **pleasure** of addressing **young
master** David of Beck Ham Street?

DAVID: **I cannot lie. It is I,** Becks. **Prithee,** hurry
and explain **thyself** as I have a photoshoot
to do with my good lady, Victoria. You
perchance know her spice shop?

forsooth	*in truth; certainly*
doublet	*close-fitting garment for upper body*
tavern	*pub or inn*
jest	*trick or game; to joke*
wherefore	*why*
'tis	*it is*
ay/aye	*yes*
alas	*expression of despair*
prithee	*please*

The wonder of Ruud

Although this appears to be an objective and well-argued piece on Ruud van Nistelrooy's prowess as a goalscorer, it is important to bear in mind that this article comes from the official Manchester United magazine, *United*.

1 The article uses a range of tables and statistics. But this is supported by some very 'loaded' language about Ruud and the other players.

Copy and complete this table with *two more* examples of loaded language:

Ruud	Comments on other players
'. . . penalties, he has missed **just one**'	'Vieri, who has managed a single goal in 883 minutes'
'**far and away** the **best** striker'	

2 Plan your own article on a favourite striker (not Ruud!). You don't need to include any tables of information, but you should just concentrate on your player's strengths and best moments.

Make notes under the following headings:

> **Title:** The Wonder of . . . *(add name of your player)*
>
> **Key strengths:** *(e.g. pace, tackling etc)*
>
> **Best goal:** *(you select)*
>
> **Rivals:** *(from UK or Europe, and how your player compares with them)*

3 Now select three top strikers from European leagues (they should be the same ones as in your notes above), and do an internet search for each one. You will probably find the best information on their clubs' official sites. Once you have found suitable sites, look for the following information and note it down:

- number of matches played: home, Europe, international
- number of goals scored: home, Europe, international
- if listed, the total number of goals scored for the club since they joined.

Add this information to your notes, in table form.

4 Now, complete your 'The Wonder of (your player)' article.

Remember to include:

- all the information from your notes
- comparison tables
- language which praises your player
- language which criticises the other three strikers.

Riot in Glasgow

1 This newspaper report from 1909 paints a very graphic picture of the riot at the match, and it is clear that the villains are the spectators. This is made very apparent by the descriptions of them and of the situation. Even the first few lines contain words such as 'cruel', rage' and 'tumult'.

Compare the behaviour of the police and the rioters by copying and completing this table with words from the text.

Police	Rioters
'beaten and injured in the most brutal and callous fashion'	'the most degraded section of the community'
'the chief sufferers of the day'	'Maddened by excitement'

2 Having completed the table, write a short summary of the *impression* given by these two sets of contrasting descriptions, supported by quotations from your table. For example, you could start:

From the descriptions given, the police come across as defenceless victims right from the start, for example, when they are described as the 'chief sufferers of the day'.

However, the rioters are presented as being almost like wild beasts, 'maddened with excitement'.

3 You will notice, too, that the style of this text contrasts with a modern-day report. Partly this is to do with the long sentences, made up of a number of clauses. For example, the long sentence which starts, 'It was generally remarked . . .' to '. . . became apparent' might be rewritten in a modern newspaper as follows:

Decent supporters tried to leave the ground when the thugs and louts started rioting.

Find another long sentence in the text, and try to put it into your own words, as if writing for a modern newspaper.

The Hillsborough disaster: 14 years on

The article looks back at the Hillsborough tragedy, and for that reason is able to recount the events that happened and their causes, as well as the aftermath and the situation now.

Look at the way the overall structure of the first part of the article has been broken down:

The headline	Sums up the article – it's an anniversary of the disaster
Paragraph 1	Deals with the 'news' (it's the anniversary) Tells us *where* it took place: Sheffield Tells us *what* happened: death of 96 people at semi-final Tells us *why* they died: 'crushed to death' Tells us *when* – 1989 Tells us *who* was involved – Liverpool and Nottingham Forest.
Paragraph 2	Single sentence for impact tells of the effect of Hillsborough: 'changed forever'.
Paragraph 3	Background on Hillsborough and 1989 programme
Paragraph 4	Warnings: looking back with hindsight at how the tragedy was caused.
Paragraph 5	More on the causes

1 Continue the table for the rest of the article, summing up what is dealt with by each paragraph of the text.

2 The writer also uses the idea of the match programme *ironically.* That is to say that with hindsight (looking back today with the knowledge of what happened) we can see how wrong and misguided the words in the programme were.

This might be called *tragic irony*. Of course, irony such as this need not always be as sad and tragic. Sometimes, ironic events can lead to humour or amusement. For example, a man has not been getting on well with his girlfriend, so he joins a dating agency. He is given the details of someone who sounds perfect for him. He arranges a blind date, but when he gets there it turns out to be his girlfriend, who has also joined the agency.

Create your own short story in which there is an *ironic event* (either sad or amusing).

3 The report deals mainly with the events at Hillsborough and how they were caused, but the second part of the article also deals with the actions of the *Sun* and, more recently, the BBC. The media clearly has a responsibility in such circumstances. How did the *Sun*, in particular, upset the relatives of the victims, and how did the paper itself suffer in return?

Pupil excluded over Beckham crop

This report focuses on a local event influenced by a national figure. In one sense, this is a minor issue, but the article does touch on some important talking-points – for example, the way young people are influenced by celebrities/role models, and also the extent to which schools should be able to decide how students dress and look.

1 Both sides of the argument are presented here. Copy and complete the chart below which lists the arguments for both sides.

For (the haircut)	Against
Gary 'fancied a change' – no big deal.	Gary 'excluded himself' as he knew what the consequences would be.

2 The article interweaves *quotations* from the key people involved with the main description of what happened. For example:

'But Ms Ward said Gary and others in his year group had already been warned about hairstyles, and called the teenager's decision to shave his head an **"act of defiance"**.'

a Find another example of quotations placed into statements like this, towards the end of the article.

b Writers can make use of quotations by *paraphrasing* (putting into their own words) what people say, but leaving some speech as it was originally.

Turn the following section from the article into a mixture of *reported speech* (what people said without the speech marks) and actual *quotation*.

<u>Original article</u>

'**I** think it's **stupid I** was sent home. A hairstyle doesn't change you, and it's better than my last one anyway, which was dyed blond with an undercut, and was a bit curly.'

Paraphrase with quotation (note how words are changed: 'I' becomes 'he' and speech marks are removed).

For example:

Gary thinks it's **ridiculous he** was sent home, and feels that . . .

Ronaldo and the World Cup Final 2002

This report gives the basic information about what happened in the final – the goals, who scored them and provided them – but very little else related to the match action. This is much more an account of how the final impacted upon two players in particular: first, Ronaldo, and second, Oliver Kahn, the German keeper.

To paint a lively and striking picture of the final, the writer uses vivid language. It's not enough to say that Ronaldo 'got rid of the bad memories of the last final'. Instead, the writer says that scoring twice and winning the match was 'a demon banished'. This is a *metaphor*, and there are many more examples of *figurative language* like this throughout the report.

1 Match up these examples of figurative language with what they are describing.

1 'a demon banished' ⟶ a) a bad memory pushed away

2 'the sparkling jewel'   b) the World Cup trophy

3 'rising like the figure of Christ overlooking the bay at Rio'   c) lack of importance of having won goalkeeper of the tournament

4 'great Bambi eyes'   d) Ronaldo as part of the Brazil team

5 'assassin's eyes'   e) the way the German players approached

6 'dead leaves in his hands'   f) Cafu, holding the World Cup

7 'crocodile-line'   g) Ronaldo's eyes

8 'a forbidden treasure, a burning sun'   h) Ronaldinho's eyes

2 Rewrite the report *without* the vivid and emotional language. Stick to the facts. To do this, first note down the information you know about the events in the match.

For example:

First goal was a result of fumble by German keeper Oliver Kahn after 68 minutes of the game. Goal scored by Ronaldo.

When you have finished, compare your version with a friend's. Does yours stick mainly to the facts – or have you left in some opinions or viewpoints?

3 Select any match of your choice (a professional game, a school game etc.). Write *two* reports: one which sticks mainly to the facts, and the second which tries to convey something of the atmosphere, the setting and the personalities.

Comparing texts

1 When you compare texts, you are looking to explore the features that make them *similar* and *different*. Texts can be similar in lots of ways. They can share the same:

- themes
- purposes
- viewpoints
- style/language
- shape/form.

It is unusual for them to share *all* of these features. Even two articles in similar newspapers on the same football match probably have different styles. At a more basic level one writer might choose to mention a specific incident in the match that the other writer leaves out.

Look at two texts from this section: **Riot in Glasgow** and **The Hillsborough disaster: 14 years on**. What can we definitely say is similar about these two texts?

They both deal with problems involving spectators at a football match.

However, the differences are more noticeable. Look again at the articles and make notes on both texts under the headings in the table that follows. The first two have been done for you.

How the texts are constructed	*Riot in Glasgow*	*Hillsborough*
The purpose of the texts	To report on the incident the day after the game and point out who was to blame	To recall the incident many years later, and remind us who was to blame
When the texts were written	1909	2003

How the texts are constructed	*Riot in Glasgow*	*Hillsborough*
The viewpoint (if any) of the writer of the article – in particular, what was said about the police and the spectators		
How the information is organised (i.e. the time order of events – just covering one single event in time, or events over a number of years?)		
The use of language (length and complexity of sentences)		
Particular uses of words/phrases		

2 You can also look for interesting similarities between texts which, on the surface, have nothing in common. Look closely at **Pupil excluded over Beckham crop** and **Ronaldo and the World Cup Final 2002**. The *differences* are fairly obvious:

Pupil excluded:

- is a web article about a schoolboy's haircut
- gives a balanced view of the two viewpoints
- has no real sense of an 'author'

- has a fairly plain and simple style of language (little, if any, figurative language)
- uses lots of direct quotation.

Ronaldo and the World Cup Final:

- is a report following the match
- gives strong support (almost worship!) for Ronaldo
- provides a strong sense of the author's view
- uses vivid, powerful language
- uses little, if any, direct quotation.

In what ways are these two pieces *similar*?

Think about what they have to say about two world-famous footballers, and their influence. Now try to turn this into a simple paragraph or two about the two texts:

The first text shows the influence of a world-famous player, David Beckham, on . . .

This is shown by . . .

Similarly, the second text also shows the influence of a world-famous player, although this time it is Ronaldo. His influence is on . . .

This is shown by . . .

---

3 Looking at the texts as a whole within this section, you can see that most are what might be called *non-literary non-fiction*. This means that they deal mainly with *information* and *facts*. They are also often *impersonal*, i.e. there is little sense of the author as a 'real person'.

Their main purpose is to *inform* and *describe,* but many texts have more than just one purpose. Such texts can also be *persuasive*, and even statistics and information can be *entertaining*, if the information interests us.

Many of the texts in this section, while including facts and information, or describing the main incidents in an event, also use quite literary techniques, such as:

- powerful, emotive language: for example, describing moments of high drama and the effects on those taking part or watching
- personal viewpoint: for example, by writing in the first person the writer gives a sense of what that person felt, how the experience changed or affected them etc.
- figurative language: for example, striking use of metaphors, similes etc.

Which, in your opinion, is the most *literary* text in this section?

Why do you think this is? Look to see if any of the techniques listed in the bullet points above occur.

Section 3
Touchlines:
Prose fiction, plays and poetry

Football, like most sports, doesn't necessarily lend itself to imaginative writing – after all, the pleasure is in the playing and watching. But football does make for great excitement and drama; there are heroic achievements and tragic failures; characters and settings; plots and sub-plots. And even those who *don't* like football usually have something to say – and what better way than through rhyme, drama or story. This section's theme is football, but it is also about how writers seek to entertain us, explore new worlds, and tell us their stories, using football as the backdrop.

Tudor football

Alexander Barclay, c.1520

The first poem in this section was written hundreds of years ago and might just as well have come from a history book, as a book about football. It provides a fascinating insight into the origins of football, but also gives us an interesting picture of Tudor life, along with spellings and vocabulary that have mostly fallen from fashion nowadays.

Eche time and season hath his delite and joyes,
Loke in the stretes, behold the little boyes,
Howe in fruite season for joy they sing and hop,
In Lent is each one full busy with his top
And nowe in winter for all the **greevous** colde
All rent and ragged a man may them beholde,
They have great pleasour supposing well to dine,
When men be busied in killing of fat swine,
They get the bladder and blowe it great and thin,
With many beanes or **peason** put within,
It ratleth, soundeth, and shineth clere and fayre,
While it is throwen and caste up in the ayre,
Eche one contendeth and hath a great delite
With foote and with hande the bladder for to smite,
If it fall to grounde, they lifte it up agayne,
This **wise** to labour they count it for no payne,
Renning and leaping they drive away the colde,
The sturdie plowmen lustie, strong and bolde
Ouercommeth the winter with driving the foote-ball,
Forgetting labour and many a grevous fall.

greevous: grievous or very serious or painful
peason: peas
wise: way, manner

What do they see in it?

Kerry Impey

It's easy to think that football appeals to everyone, especially now that many footballers are fashionable celebrities and icons. However, the day-to-day reality of football can be rather different, as this Year 7 student describes.

What do they see in it?
Standing there in the freezing cold,
Watching the ball go up and down,
Up and down. Up and down.
Then tackling one another.
How boring!
I feel sorry for the ball,
After all,
It's the thing that's going up and down,
Up and down, up and down.
And it probably has the same feeling as me,
How boring!
Why don't they just go home
And do all the housework?
But they'd probably think,
How boring!
So all they do is stand in the freezing cold,
Watching the ball go up and down,
Up and down. Up and down.
How boring!

Three lions

David Baddiel, Frank Skinner and the Lightning Seeds

Songs and chants at football grounds are part and parcel of the football experience, although many are too rude or abusive to include here. Occasionally, songs or chants designed to support a team become extremely well known. Perhaps the most famous example is the 1996 hit 'Three lions', written for the Euro '96 football tournament which took place in England. England reached the semi-finals, but long after the tournament was over, the song continued to be sung at England matches throughout the world. What was it about the lyrics that proved so popular?

It's coming home, it's coming home,
It's coming, football's coming home   (× 4)

Everyone seems to know the score,
They've seen it all before
They just know
They're so sure,
That England's going to
Throw it away
Gonna blow it away
But I know they can play,
Cos I remember . . .

Three lions on a shirt,
Jules Rimet still gleaming
Thirty years of hurt,
Never stopped me dreaming

Jules Rimet: the Jules Rimet trophy is the World Cup trophy

So many jokes, so many sneers
But all those oh-so-nears
Wear you down
Through the years
But I still see that tackle by **Moore**
And when Lineker scored,
Bobby belting the ball
And **Nobby** dancing

Three lions on a shirt,
Jules Rimet still gleaming
Thirty years of hurt,
Never stopped me dreaming

I know that was then
But it could be again

It's coming home, it's coming home,
It's coming, football's coming home.
(Repeat to fade)

Moore: Bobby Moore, England captain, 1966
Bobby: Bobby Charlton, England striker, 1966
Nobby: Nobby Stiles, England midfielder, who did a little dance at end
of the 1966 final

And Smith must score
Attila the Stockbroker

Attila the Stockbroker is a performance poet who supports Brighton and Hove Albion. At the time of writing he is their writer-in-residence, working with the club and local adults and children. He is also the club's matchday PA announcer and DJ.

In this poem, he refers back to Brighton's one and only appearance so far in an FA Cup Final, in 1983, when they held Manchester United to a 2–2 draw. However, the game is memorable for the miss by Gordon Smith which would have won the cup for Brighton. The commentator at the time said, 'And Smith must score!'. His shot was saved. United won the replay 4–0. Interestingly, and a fact that is often forgotten, is that Smith scored for Albion earlier in the game! Yet, he has never been able to forget his chance of glory.

(Brighton & Hove Albion v Manchester United, FA Cup Final, 1983 . . . our finest hour)

Five yards out, an open goal
and not a man in sight
The memory of that awful miss
still haunts me late at night . . .
Ten seconds left in extra time
and history in the making
but Smith's shot hit the goalie's legs
and now our hearts are breaking . . .

A paralytic lemming
with the skill of a dead cat
and the finesse of a hamster
could have done better than that . . .

A decomposing dogfish
wrapped in bondage head to toe
could have stuck that ball into the net . . .
but Gordon Smith? Oh no!

When Robinson broke down the left
and stuck the ball across
we knew for sure the Seagulls' win
was Man United's loss
and as old Smithy shaped to shoot
a mighty roar went up . . .
The impossible had happened.
We'd won the FA Cup!

A fleeting glimpse of glory –
alas, 'twas not to be . . .
we lost the replay 4–0:
went down to Division Three.
The one chance of a lifetime
so cruelly snatched away.
But till the white coats come for me
I'll never forget that day!

The football shirt

Linda Hoy

Novels about football are fairly common, especially for younger teenage readers. Most deal with the exploits of one youth team or another, but Linda Hoy's novel *United on Vacation* takes a slightly different approach. In the story, George, an avid Sheffield United fan, whose parents' business has gone bankrupt, wins a holiday to North Africa. There he is visiting a market stall, when a young boy, Ali, who calls George 'Jaws', recognises his shirt. Is it possible that Ali is a **Blades** fan?

Ali leads me to a small shack behind the stalls across the road. The shack is made out of palm leaves plaited together. It's about the same size as one of the stockrooms we have at school.

'Come.'

There is no door, just an opening in the wall. The room is dark because there are no windows, but Ali lights the stub of a candle.

'Come.'

In the flicker of the candlelight, I can just make out a tiny table with an enamel bowl containing a bar of soap and a razor. There is no other furniture. There are coloured blankets folded neatly on the floor. There are no beds. Sacks have been made into pillows. There is no fireplace, no bathroom, no sink. There's a curtain across part of the room. It's made from a stripy blanket and held up with nails.

'Come, Jaws.'

Ali lifts up the blanket and beckons.

Blades: Sheffield United's nickname

I stand and stare around me. I point at the empty walls. I speak slowly and carefully. 'Is this. . .' I point to Ali, '. . . where you live?'

He nods. 'Ali live here. Also,' he points to the five blankets and the five pillows by the wall. He tells me five more names.

I think of our house at home. The empty swimming pool. The jacuzzi. The dishwasher and the microwave. The conservatory. The long, winding drive. . .

'Come, Jaws.' Ali draws back the curtain and holds up the candle flame. I can hardly believe my eyes. There on the wall, fastened with drawing pins, creased and battered, is a picture torn out of a magazine. A team picture of Sheffield United.

My face breaks into a grin. 'Sheffield United,' I laugh.

'Yes,' says Ali, smiling. 'Sheffield United.'

He points at my T-shirt. 'Sheffield United.' Then he points back at the picture. 'Sheffield United.'

Both of us grin together.

I look around this tiny part of the shack. In the corner on the floor is a clean shirt, a pair of jeans and some socks. On the floor is a sack and a blanket. I stand and shake my head in amazement. This tiny section behind the curtain, this must be Ali's room, I tell myself. These are his clothes. This picture of United is the only other thing he owns.

Ali and I are strangers, but I'm aware that he's shown me something very special, very personal. The picture is his prize possession.

I think of my own room with my big comfy bed, my own bathroom, my desktop, my books. . .

I feel a kind of choking, a lump in my throat as I look round the tiny space. This is something I want to stay with me. I want the memory to stay fixed in my mind. But there is nothing else to see. Only the shadowy space with the sack, the blanket, the pillow . . . and the picture of Sheffield United.

* * *

Ali leads me back to the market stall. Before I turn to leave, he reaches out again and touches my shirt.

I smile and nod.

The stallholder beckons me across. He's collected together the painted perfume bottle that I chose, the cigarette lighter and the marzipan dates and he's wrapping them in newspaper. Of course, I can't afford to buy all three of them. I start to shake my head.

Ali grips the bottom of my shirt again and points to the parcel, nodding his head. He gabbles to the stallholder in Arabic. I don't understand what's happening now. I start to feel a bit worried. I think I ought to be getting back to Grumps and Gramps.

Ali tugs on my shirt again. 'Jaws,' he says to me. 'Jaws.'

I nod.

'Ali.' He points towards himself.

I nod again.

He points to the parcel, lifting my arm to encourage me to take it. He tugs at my shirt again. And that's when the penny drops.

My heart sinks. I start to shake my head.

Ali nods. The stallholder nods, thrusting the parcel towards me. I understand now what he's after. He wants me to give him my shirt.

I look away, embarrassed. How can I explain? How can I make him understand that this was the last shirt in the shop? This shirt cost nearly all my savings and it's the best shirt I've owned in all my life. A special holiday souvenir.

The stallholder is still thrusting the parcel towards me. It occurs to me now that he might be Ali's father. Obviously, with these items, he's trying to buy the shirt for him.

I don't know what to say. I don't know how to explain. I should have brought Gran's Sheffield Wednesday shirt with me. I wouldn't have minded trading that.

I look down at Ali, his lips squeezed tightly together as he stares up at the shirt.

The man behind the stall holds my gaze with an eager smile on his face. He points at my shirt.

I shake my head again. I look back at Ali's pleading face. I think of his ragged picture of the team, the most important thing he owns and I suddenly realise just how much the shirt would mean to him. I can buy another shirt, another time. I can go back to the Blades Shop any time I like. All I need is the money.

For Ali, this might be his only chance – the chance of a lifetime – to own a Sheffield United shirt. When I've gone, it'll be too late.

Bend it like Beckham
Narinder Dhami

This extract is from the start of the novel, *Bend it like Beckham* by Narinder Dhami, based on the well-known film of the same title. It opens with a major European match in progress on television, with a new star about to emerge.

'And it's a goal by Jess Bhamra! A superb header, beating the defender and planting the ball just out of reach past the goalkeeper. Jess Bhamra makes a name for herself at Old Trafford! Have we discovered a new star here, Gary?'

Back in the TV studios, Gary Lineker turns to Alan Hansen and John Barnes. They all look well impressed.

'Good question, Motty,' says Gary, turning to the panel. '*Could* Jess Bhamra be the answer to England's prayers, Alan?'

Alan raises his eyebrows. 'There's no denying the talent there, Gary. She's quick-thinking, comfortable on the ball, she's got awareness and vision. I tell you what, I wish she was playing for Scotland.'

Gary laughs and turns to John Barnes. 'John, do you think England have found the player to help them relive our 1966 World Cup glory?'

'No question, Gary,' says John. 'I think we've finally got the missing piece of the jigsaw. And, the best thing is, she's not even reached her peak yet.'

Gary turns to the camera. 'Now, joining us in the studio is Jess's mother, Mrs Bhamra.'

MUM?! Get out of my fantasy!

'So, Mrs Bhamra, you must be very proud of your daughter?' Gary beams.

'Not at all!' shrieks Mum. 'She shouldn't be running around with all these men, showing her bare legs to seventy thousand people. She's bringing shame on her family—' she gives the panel a filthy look '—and you three shouldn't be encouraging her.'

Gary, Alan and John look like little boys who've just been told off by their teacher.

'Jesminder, you get back home right now!' Mum rants on, pointing her finger at the camera. 'Wait till I get hold of you! Jesminder. . .'

A second later, my bedroom door crashed open.

'Jesminder, are you listening to me?' Mum demanded.

Why did she always have to interrupt at the best bits? Gary was about to interview Sven-Goran Eriksson, who was considering calling me up for the next England match.

'Jesminder, have you gone mad?' Mum pointed at the TV and glared at me. Her special *Listen to me, I'm your mother and I know best* glare. 'Football shootball! It's your sister's engagement party tomorrow, and you're sitting here watching that skinhead boy.'

She grabbed the remote control from me, and snapped the TV off. I groaned.

'Oh, *Mum,* it's Beckham's corner.'

Mum took no notice. She never does. 'Come downstairs,' she ordered me. 'Your sister's going crazy.'

Tell me something I don't know. Pinky's pretty crazy, anyway. Now, with her wedding coming up, she's a full-on lunatic. I could hear her downstairs right now, having a fit about something or other.

I stood up with a sigh. My bedroom was the only place I could really chill out, but even here I couldn't get any peace and quiet half the time. I had the room exactly how I wanted it, even though Mum never stopped moaning. Pictures of David Beckham everywhere, and my Manchester United Number 7 shirt hanging on the wall.

Beckham was my hero. OK, I know what you're thinking. Yes, he's gorgeous. You'd have to be blind not to see it. But that's not why I like him. He's a god on the football pitch. *No-one* can bend a ball like Beckham.

'I'm sick of this wedding, and it hasn't even started yet,' I muttered, staring at the poster of Becks over my bed. I talked to him all the time.

Beckham looked back at me as if he understood. He always understood. Nobody else did. Not in this house, anyway. It was just 'football shootball'. I remembered a quote by a famous Liverpool manager that I'd read the other day. *Some people think football's a matter of life and death. It's much more important than that.* That was exactly how I felt.

I went downstairs as slowly as I could. Pinky was standing in the hall, looking like she was about to rip someone's head off with her bare hands.

'Why else would she do this at the last minute?' she was screaming. 'She wants to ruin it for me. I'm telling you, Mum, she's a first-class witch.'

'Pinky!' Mum scolded, rushing down the stairs and into the kitchen. 'You've got plenty of others.'

'But it's all *planned,*' Pinky wailed. 'I need another one now.' She shot me a poisonous stare. 'Will you get a flaming move on!'

'What's going on?' I asked. It sounded as if someone had died, at the very least.

Pinky turned on me. 'Get this. Teet's sister's gone and said *she's* wearing baby pink to our engagement party now.' If looks could kill, her fiancé's sister would have dropped down dead on the spot. 'And I've got all my matching accessories and *everything.*'

I nearly said *Is that all?*, but luckily stopped myself just in time. Or it would have been *me* lying dead in the hall. 'Oh, Mum,' I groaned. 'Do I have to go shopping AGAIN?'

Mum charged out of the kitchen, shaking a carrot at me. 'My mother chose all my twenty-one dowry suits herself – and I never complained once. You girls are too spoiled.' She waved us out of the door. 'And don't forget my *dhania*. Four bunches for a pound. Oh, and some more carrots.'

This wedding was getting well out of hand, I thought, clinging to the dashboard as Pinky drove like a maniac to Southall Broadway. And we still had to get through the engagement ceremony tomorrow night first.

'We'll go to Damini's,' Pinky ordered, breezing along the Broadway like she owned it. She'd taken her denim jacket off, and in her skimpy red top, sprayed-on jeans and sunglasses, she was turning a lot of guys' heads. No-one was looking at me in my Adidas sweatpants and top. But that was the way I liked it.

My sister's the shopper from hell. We spent an hour in Daminis looking at suits. We didn't buy any of them. Then she dragged me into Ajanta Footwear to look at shoes. I didn't bother pointing out that it wasn't worth looking at shoes until we'd bought the suit. The mood Pinky was in, she'd probably have thrown me under a bus just for mentioning it.

'Oh no,' I heard Pinky mutter as we went into the shop.

Our cousins, Meena, Bubbly and Monica, were in Ajanta, trying on shoes. They're all right, I guess. If you like bubble-headed bimbos with only two things on their mind – boys and clothes. They were all wearing strappy little tops and tight jeans, and they had dyed hair with streaky highlights. They think they're the Indian version of Jennifer Aniston. They wish. I saw Pinky's face drop, then she put on this really fake smile and rushed over to them like she hadn't seen them for five years.

'Hi! *Mwah! Mwah!*'

---

dhania: coriander

There was a lot of hugging and air-kissing going on. I just stuck my hands in the pockets of my sweatpants, and tried to look invisible.

'Whatcha doin' here, man?' squealed Monica. 'You haven't left everything till the last minute, have you?'

Pinky laughed. 'Yeah, one more day of freedom!'

Monica, Bubbly and Meena laughed too, but they all looked a bit sick. They were probably wishing it was *them* getting married.

My heart sank as I saw Pinky suddenly stare Monica straight in the eye. 'When did you get your contacts?' she asked in a frosty voice.

Oh no, I thought.

Monica looked smug. 'D'ya like them? I just thought they went with my hair.'

'Oh.' Pinky went in for the kill. 'My fiancé doesn't like dyed hair.' She smirked as Monica looked furious. 'Still, can't stand here chatting all day. I'm going to Ealing for my facial. Laters.'

'Bye, Pinky, laters,' the three airheads chorused.

Pinky grabbed my arm and pulled me over to the door. 'Stupid witch,' she moaned in my ear. 'Why'd she have to go and get blue contacts? Now I can't wear mine!'

I had to bite my tongue to keep quiet. We'd be shopping for new body parts next.

The moment of contact
Christopher Kenworthy

The events in this extract from Christopher Kenworthy's short story 'Them Belgians' take place when the writer, who is in Belgium on business, is forced to stop for the night at a small town called Tournelle. The next day he finds himself near the local football stadium, and with nobody back in England to care whether he stays to see the game or not, he decides to watch it. On the way to the ground he finds himself thinking about his failed relationships, but as the match progresses his attention is drawn to one player.

The teams ran out to polite clapping, until Flensse trotted on to the pitch. He was built like a rugby player, but he also looked hollow, because his movements were so light. His skin was unaccountably brown, almost Asian in comparison to his countrymen. His nose was broken in two places, spread across a thick head. The crowd chanted: 'Ballet, Ballet.' I don't usually like football being compared to art, or dancing, or anything like that. It's just football. The way he moved, though, even when warming up, made me think his nickname didn't lose anything in translation. He was on tiptoes the whole time.

The crowd didn't throw bog rolls or bits of paper, like we used to, but flowers. Roses, carnations, even bushy chrysanthemums. Red and yellow, like the Tournelle strip. I couldn't imagine our lot chucking flowers. Too girlie for starters, and what's more, you can't nick them from the toilet. The plants didn't have quite the same travel as the soft-strong and long, but the effect was more pleasing.

Flensse never acknowledged the crowd, even though their shouts of praise were quite frantic at times. The closest he came to me was about twenty yards, and I saw him coughing up. He kept the gob in his mouth, concentrating on the ball, and just as I expected him to spit it out, his Adam's apple bulged. He swallowed his own gob. There was a tiny yet audible sigh from the crowd around me, admiring his restraint.

Tournelle had only one tactic. Pass to Flensse. He would do the rest. He was marked by half the Bruges team, but if the ball came near him, he just walked between them and took it away. His size made you expect him to lumber, but he **minced**, then moved with alarming, sharp strides and, with a tiny chipping movement, plopped it in the net time after time. You could say there was beauty in that, if you looked hard enough, but that might be distorting the truth. It was good to watch; impressive, skilful. The man was an original, but he held his moment of beauty back until the second half.

It was dark by half-time, and the air was becoming foggy. After a few minutes, I couldn't see the other side of the pitch. The floodlights didn't cut through the fog, but swelled in it, making the space in the stadium into a steady, cold flare. When the players emerged for the second half the mist was so thick they could hardly see each other. In any other country the match would probably have been called off. In Belgium they had to play on in these conditions or they'd never get through a game.

The silhouette of Flensse seemed more substantial than the rest, and where the fog slowed them like a syrup, he skipped on. At times, there were only a few players in sight, and I hardly saw the ball. It was probably the same for the players, and no goals were scored. The crowd went quiet, trying to hear where the ball was, listening for

---

minced: walking with short steps in an affected or dramatic manner

the dulled sound of the whistle, and the yelps of pain from secretive fouls.

Towards the end of the game it rained ferociously, and the fog was flattened away in seconds. The floodlights shone on the soaking grass, and the players resolved into focus. Flensse had the ball, and for a change he passed it across, ran forward, stalled to avoid offside. Then he began to run with a look of certainty that made me know he was going to score. Bruges saw it too, and ran at him from all sides. From his left the ball was lobbed clumsily across. It never hit the ground, but strummed off Flensse's right foot with a snap. It was as though two curved lines had been drawn to that exact point: the curve of the ball, and the arc of his foot. Sacred geometry. Perhaps it was the water and light on the ball, but it appeared to spark as his foot made contact. Everything about the day had led to that moment. The ball sank into the net at the same moment Flensse padded on to the ground, arms by his side, head down as though embarrassed. The others cheered and leapt, and although they danced around him, they knew better than to maul him.

When you see something beautiful, you don't celebrate or scream. You feel lonely. Beauty reminds you how much you are on your own, because there's nobody to share it with.

Afterwards, I felt quite strange and stayed in my seat until most of the crowd had gone. I had no memory of the goalies, because one had nothing to do, and the other could do nothing to stop the ball. It was only five o'clock, but so dark it felt later. I tried to pick out each spot he'd scored from; there were six patches in all, but my gaze kept returning to the place where he landed the last one.

It can only have been ten minutes later that I saw something else. Managing to get lost inside the stadium, I came out of the wrong exit, and walked round the perimeter to get back on track. I looked for a dark place in front of the lights, and guessed it would be the park. The road curved that way, so I followed, walking slowly, enjoying the rain cooling my skull.

On the corner of the main road and the park, I saw the florist's where Tournelle must have bought their flowers. It was closing for the night. The girl who worked there was taking flowers inside. She drew a bunch from its green pavement bucket, shook the sappy water off and went inside. She came back, eased the bucket over, its water sloshing into the gutter. She did this four times as I walked up. Light came from the shop windows, the pavement shining like ice. I could hear every drop, the squeak of stems as she gathered them together, and even from this distance, I saw every movement of her hair, her hands. The fifth time she came out, I saw her face.

When you see a good-looking person, what is it that stirs you, even if you've never spoken to them? Even if you stand no chance of ever smiling at them. I didn't realise at the time, but looking back, I think it was the simplicity of what she was doing, emptying water, taking in flowers. There was nothing to it, but the light and smell and the sound of her hands shaking that water. It made me feel sad for her, but I couldn't tell why. Perhaps it was the dark and cold, or the fact that I wanted to talk to her and knew I probably wouldn't.

I slowed down to get a better look. Inside, she put on a duffel coat and a satchel, turned off the light, and came out as I approached. Her hair glowed in the streetlight, and her eyelashes were stuck together with rain, making them look sparkly. She adjusted the straps on her satchel, wiped her face, and smiled.

It's easy to say that I was **deluded** about all this. A goal is a goal. A pretty person you've never spoken to is just

---

deluded: deceived or tricked

that. But I don't think so. The point is, we both turned up at that moment. I was there by mistake, in the wrong country, a day late, walking back down the wrong road. She was leaving work. Meaningless coincidence, you could say. But I can't get Flensse's goal out of my head. The geometry going on, his leg, curving and arcing with exact mathematics to intersect the line of the ball at that one moment. I'm not sure who's responsible for that sort of precision.

I almost walked past her, but stopped and smiled. It was more like a grin, and I'm surprised she didn't walk away, thinking I was weird.

What did we share? She looked up at the stadium, still not knowing I was English.

'Flensse,' I said. 'Six-nil.'

It was only a starting point, I know that. And I was brought there by chance, not effort. But when so many things come together at once, you know that something good will follow. It's the moment of contact that counts.

The story of Jorge
Simon Ings

This is part of the opening to a hard-hitting story called 'Sobras the Sacrifice' by Simon Ings, and tells the story of a young Brazilian player who tries to escape his upbringing in the slums of Rio de Janeiro. The world that is depicted is cruel and unforgiving. By the time he is eight years old Jorge has already worked in the same acid-soaked tanning plant as his father and uncle, but he fears the scars they carry, worrying that if his face is disfigured he'll never be seen on television as a professional footballer, for *futebol* is his one escape.

When Jorge is nine his father gets a job in a cementation plant in Niterói. The family – three boys and two girls and an idiot mother, **clowned** by loose scaffolding in their first year of matrimony – move to the Morro da Esperança, into the cramped attic of a shack that smells of wet mortar. There is no plaster, no flooring, and in Jorge's room, no roof.

But Jorge doesn't care about the square of corrugated tin lashed to the beams above his bed, wobbling, rusty and serrated like the sword-blade of a gutter-rat **Zeus**. Jorge doesn't care that his mother is howling in the next room, convinced the cans she collects in return for bread flee down the street and, if she catches them, take root.

Jorge cares only that this is Rio, the home of the **Maracanã**!

* * *

---

clowned: brain-damaged (by the scaffolding falling on her)
Zeus: supreme Greek god, ruler of other gods and the heavens
Maracanã: enormous football stadium in Rio de Janeiro

Jorge's father enrols Jorge in the junior team of a local football club. It is a stake a poor father often places on the future of his eldest son. If Jorge does well, the whole family will benefit. And Jorge has skill, flair, determination and speed.

Jorge's father has none of these things. Instead he loses three fingers in an industrial accident and gets religion. Every Sunday he walks into a freshly painted warehouse on the edge of town and hands half his wages to Jesus in return for a promotion that never comes.

Suddenly Jorge and his family are not just poor. They are broke. Jorge can't even afford the bus fare to the training ground. He is eleven years old. Old enough, in this city of resourceful beggar children, to stop the turn-around.

Old enough to say to his father, Not that life for me, Not tanning, cementation and wreckage and death.

No!

Futebol!

Old enough, when his dad tries to beat him, to take to the street and rob chemists' stores, mug tourists, face off kids weaker than him. True, the girl trawling the Copacabana, the *pivete* with the razor-blade who cuts off his ear, sets him back: he misses one training session.

So Jorge, unsupported and alone, beats and blunders his way through his apprenticeship and earns a transfer to the Vasco junior team. He promises to become the fastest striker in the city, which is the same as to say, the world. Rumours fill the city, earning Jorge a new name. The **Cariocas**, obsessed with *orixas*

---

pivete: young thug

Cariocas: people from Rio

orixas: saints/gods

and the spirits of animals, christen him *Potro*, 'the Foal'.

In his first game at the Maracanã, one hundred thousand people come to watch the Foal play. Jorge, turning his head to one side to hide the ragged stump of his ear, puffs out his chest and promises the longed-for cameras of Tele Globo a show to remember.

Even his mother is happy, gathering cans from the concrete terraces. Cans that lie still and patient in her grasp and, soothed by the Foal's magic, have no will to flee.

Four minutes into the second half, with the score 2–1 to Vasco, Fluminense's elderly winger mistimes his tackle and splits Jorge's shinbone into equal halves.

Jorge lies on his back and stares up into a sky made blind-spot black by flaring floodlights. A green dragonfly hovers over his head, his good fairy, perhaps, bidding him a reluctant farewell. On this hot night, its wings are twin scythes of green ice –

Then it is gone.

A spot of rain falls on his brow. Jorge thinks, dully: another christening.

The Vasco crowd is howling. They are stamping and screaming their love and concern for this new boy, this tough kid with the speed of an angel, this new **Bebeto**, this home-grown **Bebe Chorao**, this Foal.

But down there, sprawled in the magic circle of the holy green, something untoward is happening. The raindrop scours Jorge's brow with a line of fire, blessing him in the name of a deep, dark faith.

Bebeto: favourite Brazilian player from the 1990s
Bebe Chorao: baby 'cry-baby' – a reference to Bebeto who was nicknamed 'cry-baby' when he cried and refused to take a crucial penalty against Real Madrid

Not the Catholicism of his youth. Not his father's
Pentecostal bread tomorrow. Not the ragtag remnants of
Macumba, nor even **Carnaval**.

No.

Something else.

Surgeons at the General Hospital set Jorge's shinbone
badly. Jorge accepts the punishment. (Faster than Bebeto,
he'd bragged, and craftier than Pele!) His manager, blind
to the Foal's **hubris**, only laughs at the boy's remorse, and
pays for corrective surgery.

But the publicity surrounding Jorge's crippling
accident, kills the Foal as surely as a vet's bolt-gun. An
independent witness corroborates a keen-eyed chemist's
allegations, and Jorge is imprisoned on charges of armed
robbery. The prison doctors have few drugs with which to
treat the arthritic pain in his mis-set leg, pain that worsens
terribly in damp weather. And it rains and it rains and
it rains.

Pentecostal bread: holy communion bread received in Church
Macumba: form of religious worship, influenced by spiritism
Carnaval: annual carnival in Rio, with very colourful and lively parades
and processions
hubris: over-confidence, arrogance

An evening with Gary Lineker
Arthur Smith and Chris England

The play is set in July 1990. Bill and Monica are on holiday in Spain, trying to save their troubled marriage. Monica has been having an affair with Dan, a travel writer who has unexpectedly turned up at their hotel. Ian, one of Bill's colleagues from work, is also there, as is Birgitta, a German woman working in the hotel.

Bill and Dan are big football fans, and they have all been watching the World Cup semi-final between England and West Germany on television. The score is 1–1, when Birgitta suddenly comes back into the room.

(Birgitta enters and smartly turns the television off.)

BILL   What are you doing, for goodness' sake?

DAN   Birgitta!

BILL   *(trying to reach past her)* Now look, Birgitta. If you don't turn it on. . .

BIRGITTA   What? Will you hit me?

BILL   What?

BIRGITTA   Monica is unhappy.

DAN   I'm unhappy. You've turned the World Cup off.

(Monica enters.)

BILL   Monica. . . *(indicates TV.)*

BIRGITTA   I'm going for a walk, Ian.

IAN   Perhaps **Graeme Souness** would like to go with you.

Graeme Souness: former Scottish footballer with whom Birgitta had a drink, earlier in the play

BIRGITTA	*(grabbing him by the wrist)* Ian, I'm going for a walk.
IAN	All right, I'm coming.

(Birgitta and Ian leave.)

MONICA	Bill. There's something I have to tell you.
BILL	I know. Turn the telly on.
MONICA	I've been seeing Dan.

(Dan groans and covers his eyes.)

BILL	I know. Turn the telly on.
MONICA	Dan?
DAN	Monica.
MONICA	Aren't you going to say something?
DAN	Turn the telly on.
MONICA	No. No no no. You're going to decide this for yourselves. You're not going to let twenty-two complete strangers two thousand miles away determine whether you're happy or miserable. It's my turn. You talk about this, it's your lives, your real lives, and whatever you decide we're going to do will be all right by me. I'm surrendering myself this time. I don't want to watch the match, just tell me the result.

(Monica goes out onto the balcony. Dan and Bill avoid eye contact awkwardly for a moment or two, then both start talking at the same instant.)

BILL	You first.
DAN	No, you.
MONICA	*(on the balcony, to herself)* It's just tossing a coin, that's what it is. My mother used to say:

'If you really can't tell what you want to do,
just toss a coin.' Then if you find yourself
saying 'OK, best of three' – then you know
what it is you really want.

(Back inside the room.)

BILL   I was just going to say, a thing that Monica
always says.

DAN   What?

BILL   She always says that men, when men get
together, they never talk about the things that
they care about, about their emotions, they
just talk about football.

DAN   That's rubbish, isn't it?

BILL   Yeah, it's rubbish.

(Pause.)

DAN   That was a goal, Lineker's goal, wasn't it?

BILL   Yeah, just swept it past two of them and
tucked it in. Great goal. Our goal. It'll be in
the title sequence of *Grandstand* into the
21st century, that goal.

(Dan does a cursory bit of acting out the goal.)

DAN   It will, it will. . . See, he went past them, then
he put it behind them. It was a striker's goal. . .

(Another pause.)

BILL   You see, what she doesn't realise, Monica, is
that the things that men care about, that really
matter, that they really get emotional about
. . . they *are* football.

DAN   Exactly. We've got to think what's really
important here. . .

BILL   It's extra time in the World Cup semi-final.
       I can't believe she turned it off, I mean, what
       are we, kids?

DAN   No, we're grown men, we can sort this out
       between us. No need to get hysterical.

BILL   Absolutely not.

DAN   Let's just face the facts, deal with the
       practicalities. . .

BILL   It's England in the semi-final of the World
       Cup. I can't believe she switched that off.

DAN   And Spanish commentary as well. How are
       we going to know if they scored while we
       weren't watching?

BILL   Exactly! Exactly!

DAN   We could just switch it on again. . . ?

BILL   She'd hear.

DAN   Sound right off?

BILL   No, she'd hear, she'd hear.

DAN   She's outside.

BILL   All right, switch it on then.

MONICA'S   *(from the balcony)* Don't you dare!
VOICE

BILL   See?

DAN   God! I can't stand this. Look. I've been
       sleeping with Monica, and I'm sorry. I'll jump
       off the balcony if you want. I will. Just say
       the word.

       (Bill shakes his head.)

DAN   Did you know before?

BILL   I wondered. Something you said earlier on,
       when Germany scored.

DAN   Huh? Anyway I know this is embarrassing, but you decide what you want to do, between the two of you. I think I ought to find another publisher, just to save, you know, it's embarrassing for you. . .

BILL   Well, there's no need. . .

DAN   Not Ian. You know I wouldn't do that, don't you? You know me, don't you?

(Bill shrugs. Pause.)

DAN   What's going to happen?

BILL   Don't know.

DAN   Telly on and find out?

BILL   *(momentarily distracted, but then)* . . . yeah.

(They switch the television on. Monica screams in frustration. After a moment or two she comes in and watches them.)

DAN   What's going on, they're all sitting down. . . ?

Arrival
Ben Harris

The following script extract is taken from the seventh series of Sky Television's *Dream Team*, which is built around fictional football club Harchester United. The extract deals with the arrival back in England of a star player, Luke Davenport.

Dream Team VII, Episode 2

<u>INT. EAST MIDLANDS AIRPORT (ARRIVALS) – DAY</u>

Day four for this episode starts here.

NOTE: TO BE FILMED IN THE STILL BAR AT THREE MILLS.

There's a buzz of anticipation in the air as we track across a line of photographers all with their heavy-duty cameras lined up (as if they are behind a goal in a European final) – something serious is about to go down here.

An attractive female broadcaster holding a microphone has her hair done by a make-up girl.

SKYSPORTS PRESENTER: *(of the hair)* Just make sure it's right.

Two pretty teenage girls hurry up to one of the many waiting hacks.

GIRL 1: Is it true? Is he coming?

HACK: *(nods)* Should be here any minute.

GIRL 2:   *(trying not to scream)* Oh my god.

On the two excited girls and then . . . cut to:

<u>INT. EAST MIDLANDS AIRPORT (CONCOURSE) – DAY</u>

Day four.

'Pick up the pieces' by Average White Band kicks in.

And we go into slow motion as we see. . .

Finely tailored bespoke Italian trouser leg falling onto beautifully crafted leather shoes walking along.

*A heavily **iced-up** hand undoes a button on the long leather coat.*

The hand then pushes the dark sunglasses back into the correct position and takes the hand of his walking companion – the finely manicured nails do not go unnoticed.

We see the lady's long shapely legs as the couple walk past the camera – and we see the passers-by follow the glamorous couple with their stares.

Cut to:

<u>INT. EAST MIDLANDS AIRPORT (ARRIVALS) – DAY</u>

Day four.

The waiting press and fans go mad as the couple come into view.

---

iced-up: covered in jewellery

Luke Davenport is back on English soil.

(Beautiful female companion to be confirmed from a long list of interested parties.)

JOURNOS: Luke! Luke!

They jostle to be as close to him as possible. The lady broadcaster forces her way to the front.

SKYSPORTS PRESENTER: Luke, what you doing back in England?

We see Luke's face in close up for the first time. He's as good-looking as you just knew he would be. Better even.

LUKE: I'm going to a wedding.

We then see a shot of his impossibly beautiful travel companion.

SKYSPORTS PRESENTER: You two tying the knot?

LUKE: No.

He flashes his trademark million-dollar smile at the camera.

LUKE: I'm the best man.

The lady broadcaster melts. The two girls from earlier rush up bearing a piece of paper and a pen. . .

GIRL 2: Luke, can you . . . please. . .

Almost without looking he takes it, signs it and hands it back. We see a snatched

*close-up of the signature – just the letters
'LD' artily intertwined.*

*The girls fall away, staring disbelievingly
at the signature.*

SKYSPORTS
PRESENTER: Are you happy in Barcelona?

LUKE: It has its advantages.

SKYSPORTS
PRESENTER: Any truth in the rumour you're re-signing
for Man U?

LUKE: You'll have to ask Sir Alex about that.

SKYSPORTS
PRESENTER: Will you be seeing Arsène Wenger while
you're here?

He stops walking. Ponders.

LUKE: I'll see if I can fit him in.

*The onlookers laugh. Luke kisses beautiful
woman on the lips, the cameras flash, and
Luke walks on.*

Activities

Tudor football

1 Look at the first two lines of the poem. List any words that are spelled differently nowadays (for example, *eche* = *each*) and write down their modern spellings.

Which one of these words has become *more* difficult to spell nowadays because of the silent letters that have been added?

2 There are a number of grammatical differences between many of the lines and how the text would be written now. For example, 'When men *be busied*' would now be written as 'When men *are busy*'.

Sometimes the order of a line is different. How would the following line be written today?

'All rent and ragged a man may them beholde.'

('rent' = 'torn', 'beholde' = 'see')

3 The text makes it clear that football is a winter game, and is played by 'plowmen'. What do we find out about how a football is made?

4 Looking at the text as a whole, write a short prose piece saying what sort of image the poem gives us of football in 1520?

5 Write your own poem about football nowadays. It must:

- have 20 lines
- be written in rhyming couplets (*joyes/boyes*)
- contain references to how the football is made (in the Far East? Sold in a sports shop?)
- describe a typical match
- start with the lines: 'Every new soccer season has its ups and downs' (or 'highs and lows').

What do they see in it?

Kerry Impey's simple poem conveys the feelings of someone who just cannot see the attraction in football. Essentially, her objections boil down to three things:

- it's freezing cold
- it's boring
- it's pointless (unlike 'housework').

1 How does Kerry convey how boring the game is by her use of language?

2 Now write a short story told from the point of view of someone who is dragged along to watch a game by someone who loves football – a friend, boyfriend or girlfriend. In the story 'you' go along because you don't wish to hurt your friend's feelings, but the experience is terrible.

The game is not a glamorous Premiership one, but a local match on a playing field. As in Kerry Impey's poem it is winter and 'freezing cold'.

Use this plan, if you wish, before you start writing.

Who is your friend/boyfriend/girlfriend and **why are they involved** in the match (player? fan? coach?)

Details of **where** the match takes place (setting? weather? surroundings?)

Other people at match (old man walking his dog? rude opposing fans?)

Conversations you have and with whom (argument with friend? pretending to like the game to someone you fancy?)

What happens at the **end** (do you walk off? end up enjoying the game?)

Note: make sure you use plenty of details to create a vivid picture in the reader's mind. Don't just tell the reader how you feel.

Three lions

This song was penned for the Euro '96 football tournament which took place in England, hence the opening lines, 'It's coming home. . .', which also refer to the fact that football was invented in England, and that England last won a major trophy in 1966, and therefore success has been 'away' since then.

1 In the first verse, the songwriters use a play on words:

  'Everyone seems to know the score/They've seen it all before'

  What does 'know the score' mean in this context?

2 A pop/football song is bound to have quite a few informal/chatty words and phrases in it. Here are three from the song. What do they mean?

  - 'throw it away'
  - 'oh-so-nears'
  - 'belting' (the ball)

3 Compose your own football song/chant for your favourite team. It must follow these conventions:

  - have at least two verses and a chorus
  - mention players from the team
  - make some reference to 'glory days from the past' (i.e. getting promoted, avoiding relegation. . .)

4 When you have composed the song/chant, perform it in front of your group or class. Decide which ones work best, and why. Is it because:

  - they are funny?
  - rude about other teams?
  - have good rhymes and choruses that are easy to remember?

And Smith must score

This humorous poem works because it contains key features common to much comic writing:

- it deals with someone's misfortunes
- it has amusing, silly descriptions (and is rude about someone)
- it uses exaggerated ideas.

1 Read the poem again, then write answers to the following questions.

   a Whose misfortune does it mainly deal with? (Think carefully, this may not be as obvious as it appears.)

   b What silly descriptions are there of Gordon Smith? Find at least two. Why do these silly metaphors work?

   c The poem ends with an exaggerated idea. What does the poet say will happen to him one day?

2 The structure of the poem

Many comic or light-hearted poems use a fairly strict rhyme and rhythm structure.

   a Read the poem aloud, and see if you can identify whether the lines have a regular rhythm.

   b Now look at the **rhyme scheme** – the pattern of rhymes.

- Does every line rhyme with another?
- If not, which lines *don't* rhyme?

3 Prepare a rehearsed reading of the poem with a friend or in a group.

- Select which lines – or parts of lines – each of you is going to read.
- Decide what emphasis you will put on important or funny lines, e.g. 'a DECOMPOSING dogfish!'.

You should also decide on changes in tone of voice: disgust? excitement? anger?

Now perform your version of the poem. Afterwards, evaluate your performance.

- Did you manage to convey the feelings of the poet?
- Did you make it interesting and varied to listen to?

The football shirt

1 Stories tend to work well when the main character or characters are forced to make choices, or are confronted by situations that make them think again about themselves and their lives. In the extract from Linda Hoy's novel, both these things occur.

    a What is the choice that George has to make? Why is it difficult for him?

    b What do you think he decides to do?

2 This text is all about *parallels* – and how George draws them between his life and Ali's. To start with, this is done by focusing on individual details about Ali's house and way of life. From these details the writer suggests a great deal. For example, the fact that there is only a curtain across the room suggests that Ali has little, if any, privacy of his own in the 'house'.

What is suggested by the following details?

- Ali lighting a candle.
- Five blankets and five pillows by the wall.
- The shack is 'about the same size as one of the stockrooms' at school.
- No bathroom or sink.
- George thinking about his 'big comfy bed', the 'swimming pool' etc.

3 There is a danger that Ali may come across as a stereotype of a poor but decent North African in this story. Look at this information.

- He lives in a shack and shares with lots of members of his family.
- They appear to have no running water, electricity etc.
- His dad runs a stall, and George has to barter his shirt.
- George is seen as a rich Westerner.
- Ali mispronounces 'George' in a comical way, as 'Jaws'.
- Ali supports an English team, not a local team.

a Does this make the story (what you have read of it) more or less interesting?
b What would the story have been like if Ali's living conditions had been more 'modern'?
c How would the story have been different if Ali had been less pleasant and had tried to get George's shirt in another way?

Bend it like Beckham

1 This is the beginning of the novel based on the film. Like many stories, the opening sets up a number of the key issues and storylines that will become important later. Here are some of these issues. Find evidence for each one and make a note of it in a table like the one below. You can use either *direct quotations*, or *paraphrase* what is in the extract.

Issue	Evidence from opening
Jess's dreams of being a footballer	Jess scoring an all-important goal in her fantasy
How Jess is different from her sister (and cousins/friends)	
Jess's mother's disapproval of her lifestyle	

2 The picture painted of Pinky (Jess's sister) in this opening is especially vivid.

a How does the writer describe her? Find a range of quotations describing:

- what she says, and how she speaks, for example, 'Pinky wailed'
- how she behaves
- what she looks like.

b Once you have this information, draw conclusions about the sort of person she is, and the impression we get of her. For example, does she come across as gentle and considerate?

c Then use the following frame to help shape an account
   of Pinky's character.

> In this extract, the impression given of Pinky is that she . . .
>
> This is shown by . . .
>
> In addition, she appears to be . . .
>
> which is in direct contrast with Jess, who . . .

The moment of contact

There are some incredibly vivid descriptions in this extract. The whole structure is built around two key descriptions, which complement each other: the description of Flensse, the Tournelle player, and the girl in the flower shop. In each case, the level of detail is vitally important.

1 First look carefully at the description of the moment the ball strikes Flensse's foot when he scores, starting from the words, 'From his left the ball was lobbed…'

    a What verb does the writer use to describe the way the ball leaves his foot?

    b What 'appears' to happen as a result of the water and light?

    c What two words in a sentence of their own does the writer use to describe the way the way the two lines (the curve of the ball and the arc of his foot) meet?

2 Another unique element of the description of Flensse when he first appears is the *juxtaposition* (the placing together) of two elements of his appearance which would normally appear to contradict each other. The description relates to his build and weight. Can you find it?

3 Finally, look at the description of the girl. She is performing a simple action, and it is described by the writer in plain sentences with occasional details (such as the pavement 'shining like ice').

Write your own description of someone watching someone else performing a very simple task or action. Make sure you include *simple sentences* describing the *process* he or she is undertaking. The verbs you use must be selected precisely. Remember to include one or two details, for example, like the 'squeak of stems' or the 'sappy water'.

Here are some ideas:

- An older woman watching a child in the park throwing bread to the ducks.
- A teenage girl watching a male window cleaner washing the outside of an office building.
- A football scout watching a young player practising free kicks on his own in the park.

The story of Jorge

Although this is only an extract from a longer story, we are given a taste of what is to happen later on.

1 Predicting

    a Go through the text and make a brief list of what happens to Jorge and his family (in the order in which it happens). The list of events has been started for you below.

> - Years before, mother brain-damaged by loose scaffolding
> - Father, uncle and Jorge work in a tanning factory
> - At age nine, Jorge and family move (father gets job in cementation plant)

    b Having listed the events in Jorge's life, what direction do you suspect his life is going in?

2 Themes

Even in such a short extract, certain themes seem to be emerging. One of these relates to 'faith' and a belief in something else to help you survive.

For example:

Jorge's father hands over money to a religious group of some sort, but he doesn't get the promotion he prays (and pays) for.

What other examples are there in this extract of references to gods and faith? Are they presented by the writer as good or bad omens?

3 A pretty dreadful image is presented of life for a Brazilian child growing up in the slums or shanty towns. To what extent is this a true reflection of the background of top South American footballers? Research the life of Maradona, and find out about his early years. Does it have anything in common with Jorge's?

4 In question 1b you were asked what might happen later in the story. Write a plot summary of the rest of the story, with one simple sentence for each new event or incident.

For example:

Jorge is released from prison but can't find work, so starts hanging round the Maracanã stadium and begins begging.

An evening with Gary Lineker

1 a Divide up the roles in the play and perform it in small groups. Get one person to read the stage directions.

 b Once you have done this, review what you know about the way a play script is set out. Make brief notes on:

- layout
- punctuation
- staging.

2 a From your reading, what impression have you gained of each of the characters? Write down at least two *adjectives* to describe each one:

For example:

Ian is **thick-skinned**, **uninterested** in football.

 b Now decide how you would play Monica. Look again at the lines she speaks, and make notes on:

- how she would move
- how she would speak.

For example:

MONICA: Aren't you going to say something?

Monica stands with hands on hips. Stares straight at Dan.

 c How would Monica's movements contrast with those of Dan and Bill?

3 Monica has left Dan and Bill to sort out their feelings by themselves, and to resolve the issue of Dan having cheated on Bill. Look at the conversation between the two men while the television is off. Is Monica right that men can't talk about 'their emotions', 'only football'?

Think about your friends. Write a short piece for a teenage magazine, saying whether you believe that boys *can* talk about emotions and feelings, or if they really are more fixated on sports, hobbies etc. You can choose to make it amusing and entertaining, or give a more serious account.

Arrival

Writing for television is a skill in its own right. The skill of the television scriptwriter is to convey snapshot images and the feel of a series of shots in writing. In this extract from a TV series, notice how much effort is put into what the viewer *sees*, not just what is *said* by the characters.

1 Look at the opening to the extract on page 105. We are given three visual descriptions of different people or groups.

    a Who are these three different people/groups?
    b What do we find out about what they are doing?
    c In contrast, there is only one short line of speech. Can you find it?

2 The effort put into what the viewer sees is made even clearer on the next page with the detailed description of the player arriving.

How does the writer convey what Luke Davenport is like? Find at least three examples, and explain what each one tells us.

For example:

'He flashes his trademark million dollar smile at the camera.'

This tells us that Luke is used to handling the media. In addition, the use of the word 'trademark' suggests that Luke is almost like a brand or a product, even though he has created this image himself.

Comparing texts

Compare two prose fiction pieces

The story of Jorge and **The moment of contact** both deal with football players in foreign countries, but apart from that there are probably more differences than similarities in the two story extracts.

1 Look at the following question:

> *Football has been described as 'The beautiful game'. Looking at these two story extracts, do you think this is a good description?*

How would you answer this? Below is one answer plan you could follow.

Paragraph 1: Without referring to these two stories, say whether *you* think 'The beautiful game' is a suitable description.

In my opinion, **The beautiful game** *is not a great description of football generally because when you are playing in heavy mud in the middle of November . . .*

Paragraph 2: Write about the first story, and mention any references to 'beauty'.

In **The moment of contact** *there are moments, however, when the game – and the players in it – seem almost beautiful, for example when . . .*

Paragraph 3: Now link this to the other extract:

There are even brief moments of 'beautiful' football in **The story of Jorge***, for example, when . . .*

Paragraph 4: Start to look at differences between the two.

However, the optimism of the first story links the beautiful goal with the beautiful girl. Something good comes from the match. In contrast, when Jorge has his moment of beauty . . .

2 Either continue these paragraphs, or write your own in answer to the question.

Compare 'An evening with Gary Lineker' with 'Arrival'

Although both these texts are scripts, there are many differences between them, due to the fact that the first is a stage play, in which the audience is still and watching the whole stage, and the second is a television series, with the camera in charge, telling you where to look.

This means that there are significant differences in the stage directions and in the style.

Here are some key features of **An evening with Gary Lineker**:

- names of characters on left-hand side of page
- no speech marks
- present tense for actions/stage directions
- proportion of speaking to stage directions – approx. 80 per cent to 20 per cent (in this example)
- we learn most about the characters from what they say
- this scene is relatively 'inactive' – most characters sitting down and talking.

1 Make a similar list of features for **Arrival**.

- names?
- use of speech marks?
- use of tenses?
- proportion of speaking/stage directions/camera shots?
- how do we find out about characters?
- how active or inactive are the scenes?

2 Are there any other key similarities and differences between the extracts? For example, do the characters talk in similar ways?

3 When you have finished, try transposing either the *Dream Team* script or part of the Gary Lineker extract into prose. To do so, you will need to:

- remove character names, stage directions etc
- decide from what perspective the story is told (i.e. first person by Luke?)
- add further detail and description of settings.

Section 4

Reading the game:
Articles, reflections and interviews

In this section, we take a look at issues arising from football, and in particular, the effect of football on society, whether this relates to the problem of hooliganism or in the way football is shaping fashions and attitudes. By and large, the extracts are taken from feature articles or interviews, reporting not on instant news stories, but reflecting people's experiences and views on a wide range of subjects.

They said what?
Various

The things said by managers, players and commentators are often more entertaining than the games themselves. The slip-ups – or occasional deliberate attempts at humour – are probably a result of the fact that we hear and see what people say 'live': in the heat of the moment. Those involved with football rarely have time to go away and think through what they should say before someone thrusts a microphone in front of them.

Metaphors and more

'The way Terry Venables sometimes plays the team in his Christmas tree formation leaves me alone up front but that never bothers me … it is nice to have some company, though.'
Alan Shearer (on the then England manager)

'No one can accuse me of diving because I can't swim'
Dean Holdsworth

'Butcher goes forward as Ipswich throw their last trump card into the fire'
Bryon Butler (commentator)

'He knows that the pressure will be off and he'll be holding all the aces when the cards come out. When snooker balls are pocketed the Spanish will be in his'
Vinny Jones (on Terry Venables)

'Runners up at Wembley four times – never the bride always the bridegroom, Leicester.'
Peter Jones (commentator)

'I wish Glenn luck, but he is putting his head in the frying pan'
Ossie Ardiles (on Glenn Hoddle's application for the England manager's job)

Getting your point across

'We were taken completely by surprise by the fact that 20,000 wanted to get in. This will never happen again as long as I'm involved in Bristol City'
Scott Davidson (Bristol City director)

'We can beat anyone on our day – so long as we score'
Alex Toten (Kilmarnock manager)

'Andy should be hitting the target from those distances, but I'm not going to single anyone out'
Sir Alex Ferguson (on Andy Cole)

'You're never going to win anything with kids'
Alan Hansen (after a youthful Manchester United team are beaten 3–1 by Aston Villa on the opening day of the season – the only goal scored by a lad called D. Beckham)

'Alan Ball has been given Manager of the Month. What month I'm at a loss to imagine. Maybe they gave it to him belatedly for July – before the season started.'
Jimmy Greaves (on the then Manchester City manager)

'Any of these four countries could still qualify. And I'm sure we'll complicate that for you later.'
Des Lynam (commentator)

'I think you and the referee were in a minority of one, Billy'
Jimmy Armfield (commentator)

Darran Medley, kit designer
Simon Inglis

The importance of the 'right' clothing in football is obvious; whether it is Alex Ferguson complaining that his players couldn't see each other when wearing the grey away strip when they lost 6–3 to Southampton, or the claim that teams who wear all-white tend to win more games (e.g. Real Madrid), the issue of football fashion goes beyond the change from baggy shorts to tight to baggy again. This web article describes the influence of kit designer, Darran Medley.

DARRAN MEDLEY
KIT DESIGNER

'When designing football shirts, you're dealing with a property which is culturally important to so many people worldwide.'

Unsung creator Darran is International **Apparel** Director at Umbro, the Cheshire-based kit manufacturers who currently supply Manchester United and England. Even if you don't recall the name Umbro – coined by founder Harold Humphreys in 1924 from the words Humphrey Brothers – you'll recognise the company's double-diamond logo. It currently adorns the shirts of some 30–40 national and club teams, among them Norway, Chile, Ireland, Chelsea and Celtic. During the 1966 World Cup, 15 of the 16

Apparel: clothing

entrants wore Umbro, including England, whose red shirts in the final have since attained **iconic** status. Another classic is the yellow and green shirt worn by Brazil from 1954–1994. As Umbro are quick to note, all Brazil's World Cup triumphs were achieved in Umbro shirts.

So how does a new kit design come about?

Darran leads a team of four designers. Typically, they draw up ten designs for each new shirt. 'In the 1990s there was a tendency to appeal to the fashion market, to design shirts that would go well with jeans,' explains Darran. 'Now we try more to retain the traditional format, but interpret it in a contemporary way without alienating fans. For ideas we look at all areas of the design spectrum: cars, household items, menswear and sports fashions. But the difference when designing football shirts is that you're dealing with a property which is culturally important to so many people worldwide.'

Choice of material is also significant. Manchester United's current shirts are made from a newly invented textile called

iconic: representing or symbolising something

Sportwool, consisting of polyester and **Merino** wool. This was chosen in response to the two main concerns of players; that the shirt feels lightweight and does not absorb moisture.

From ten initial prototypes, Darran's team selects two or three to be made up by Umbro's garment technologists. Once the players have tried out the options – wearing the material in training is a major test – a final choice can be made. Darran's team works on 30–40 designs per year, resulting in the manufacture of around two million strips every season, mostly in the Far East.

Darran's favourite shirts? Not surprisingly he opts for one of Manchester City's, from the early 1970s (a sky-blue shirt with a white crew neck and cuffs). Despite his allegiance, he also loved the controversial all-black away kit designed for Manchester United in 1992 (which forced referees to don green shirts). Another favourite is the new Umbro England shirt, which introduces a red stripe down the left, backing the familiar three lions crest.

The worst? Undoubtedly the printed Arsenal away strip of the early 1990s. 'A mess!' exclaims Darran.

As to the future, he points to an innovative reversible shirt, now sported by Manchester United away from home. White on one side, gold on the other, it offers two kits for the price of one. He also believes we could soon see all-in-one kits, based on the figure-hugging Lycra suits now common in athletics. These might not catch on amongst fans, but they would cut out shirt-tugging at a stroke.

Most fans fancy themselves as a kit designer. When Umbro ran a competition with the *Sunday Mirror* newspaper for a new Manchester United design, they were swamped by 50,000 entries. So, does Darran have any tips for any would-be designers?

'Above all, some colours just don't work in football,' he advises. 'Silver is difficult, pastels are tough, but brown is a shocker! The best shirt is one that is striking, modern and refreshing.'

Merino: a breed of sheep with very fine, high-quality wool

Laura Green,
painter of football grounds
Simon Inglis

This web article, also by journalist Simon Inglis, introduces Laura Green, whose main passion in life appears to be painting football grounds, although, as the article points out, she's a pretty mean footballer herself!

'People who are interested in football are very rarely interested in art.'

Ever heard the term 'groundhopper'? A groundhopper is someone whose hobby – passion even – is to visit football grounds. Big ones, small ones. Old ones, new ones. Football grounds near to home, football grounds abroad. Almost any sort will do as long as it has an enclosed pitch and a set of goalposts.

Groundhoppers come in all types and ages, but there is one characteristic they all share. They are all, without exception, male.

Or at least they were until the recent emergence of a rather unusual 22-year-old artist, Laura Green. Laura is so **enamoured** with football grounds that during her last four years' training at the Birmingham Institute of Art and Design, in England, she has painted little else.

'I am pretty fixated on football stadiums,' she freely admits at the opening of this year's Bloomberg New Contemporaries exhibition. The annual show, first staged in 1949 to offer a platform for emerging artists from British colleges, features seven of Laura's most recent paintings. Among them are striking, vibrant images of stands at

---

enamoured: liking or loving something or somebody

British clubs such as Watford, Nottingham Forest and Villa Park, alongside more abstract general views of Wembley and Old Trafford. Always shown empty, the stands are depicted more as blocks or stripes of colour. Laura likens them to tribal flags, reflecting the fans' own allegiance to their team colours and home ground.

As you might imagine, at first not all her friends and tutors understood her choice of subject. 'It does take a bit of explaining, especially for a girl,' she says, somewhat **superfluously**. 'If I was a boy it would be more like painting cars, a boyish hobby. But as I'm a girl I think it makes people stop and ask themselves why I should want to do it, and so they then start to think more about the subject.'

Laura herself has been thinking of football and looking at stadiums ever since she attended her first Arsenal match at the age of seven. She's hardly missed a game since, regarding Highbury as her second home. Nor is she merely an observer. In her last season playing for her university women's team she notched up five goals.

'I know it's a huge generalisation but people who are interested in football are very rarely interested in art. So with my work I'm trying, consciously or subconsciously, to bring the two together. It forces my friends to react to art. Because it's about football they're automatically interested.'

Whilst out at grounds, sketching and taking photos, Laura does get some funny looks though. At Old Trafford she wrapped herself in a huge sheet of transparent **acetate**. With a felt pen she then traced the outline of the stadium on the acetate, as if immersing herself in a giant fish-eye lens. The resultant smear of red, green and blue may not be immediately recognisable as Old Trafford. But it feels like Old Trafford.

---

superfluously: more than necessary, extra
acetate: smooth, shiny, man-made material

Now that's she graduated, Laura refuses to stop. 'I'm aiming to paint as many stadiums as I can around the world. You can never say never, but the way I feel at the moment I can't see myself painting anything else.'

Hating football

Andrew O'Hagan

It is easy to assume that everyone loves football, and that football can even provide artists and designers with great inspiration. Of course, there are plenty who wish it had never existed. In this magazine article, writer Andrew O'Hagan describes his reasons for hating football.

I can tell you the exact moment when I decided to hate football for life. It was 11 June 1978 at 6.08 p.m. Scotland were playing Holland in the first stage of the World Cup Finals in Argentina. It happened to be the day of my tenth birthday party. My mother had to have the party after my actual birthday owing to a mistake involving a cement-mixer and the police, but the party was called for that afternoon, and the cream of St Luke's Primary School turned up at 4 p.m., armed with Airfix battleships and enough £1 postal orders to keep me in sherbet **dib-dabs** for a month.

Things started to go badly the minute my father rolled into the square in a blue Bedford van. He came towards the house in the style of someone in no great mood for ice-cream and jelly, and within minutes, having scanned the television pages of the *Daily Record*, he threw the entire party out of the living room – Jaffa Cakes, Swizzle Sticks, cans of Tizer, the lot – all the better to settle down to a full 90 minutes with Ally's Tartan Army, now taking the field in Mendoza.

A full cast of Ayrshire **Oompa-Loompas** (myself at the head) was then marched upstairs to a requisitioned

---

dib-dabs: sweets for dipping in sherbet
Oompa-Loompas: an imaginary race of tiny people from *Charlie and the Chocolate Factory*

boxroom, where several rounds of pass-the-parcel proceeded without the aid of oxygen. I managed to eat an entire Swiss roll by myself and take part in several **sorties** of kiss, cuddle or torture before losing my temper and marching to the top of the stairs. From there, looking through the bars, I could see the television and my father's face. Archie Gemmill, at 6.08, wearing a Scotland shirt with the number 15 on the back, puffed past three Dutch defenders and chipped the ball right over the goalie's head. The television was so surprised it nearly paid its own licence fee, and my father, well, let's just say he stood on the armchair and forgot he was once nearly an altar-boy at St Mary's.

My school chums were soon carried out of the house on stretchers, showing all the signs of a good time not had, by which point my mother was mortified and my father was getting all musical. 'We're here to show the world that we're gonnae do or die,' he sang **unprophetically**, 'coz England cannae dae it coz they didnae qualify.' My birthday was spoiled, and I decided always to hate football and to make my father pay. I had a hidden stash of books in a former breadbin upstairs – the revenge of the English swot! – and I went out to the swingpark to read one and to fantasise about becoming the West of Scotland's first international male netball champion.

Hating football was a real task round our way. For a start, my brothers were really good at it; the fireplace had a line of gold and silver strikers perched mid-kick on **alabaster** bases, and they turned out to be the only part of the fireplace where my father wouldn't flick his cigarette ash. For another thing, I went to a school where

---

sortie: an exploratory raid and return to base in battle; a short trip, especially to an unfamiliar place
unprophetically: not being able to foretell or predict events
alabaster: white, chalky stone, often used for ornaments

Mr Knocker, the teacher, was football-daft, and he'd sooner you packed in Communion than afternoon football. But Mark McDonald – my fellow cissy – and I broke his spirit after he gave us new yellow strips to try on. We **absconded** from the training session and stretched the shirts over our knees, all the better to roll down Toad Hill in one round movement before dousing the shirts in the industrial swamp at the bottom. The destruction of footballing equipment was beyond the pale: we were too young for Barlinnie Prison, so we got banned to Home Economics instead and were soon the untouchable kings of **eggs Mornay**.

My father gave up on me. Mr Knocker put me down for a hairdresser and a Protestant.

---

absconded: left secretly (to avoid punishment)
eggs Mornay: eggs in a cheese sauce

Among the thugs
Bill Buford

Of course, there are plenty of things to make the non-football fan justified in hating football. Perhaps top of the list is the issue of hooliganism. This is an extract from an article by Bill Buford, who decided to go 'undercover' in Italy with England fans. In this extract they are moving through the city of Turin, smashing anything in sight. Many people have already been viciously beaten, and buildings and vehicles attacked. But the Italian police soon arrive.

We moved on.

I felt weightless. I felt nothing would happen to me. I felt that anything might happen to me. I was looking straight ahead, running, trying to keep up, and things were occurring along the dark **peripheries** of my vision: there would be a bright light and then darkness again and the sound, constantly, of something else breaking, and of movement, of objects being thrown and of people falling.

Is it possible that there were simply no police?

Again we moved on. A bin was thrown through the display-window of a car dealer, and there was another loud crashing sound. A shop: its door was smashed. A clothing shop: its window was smashed, and one or two English supporters lingered behind to loot from the display.

I looked behind me and I saw that a large vehicle had been overturned – was it a lorry? – and that further down the street flames were issuing from a building. I hadn't seen any of that happen: I realised that there had been

---

peripheries: edges or boundaries

more destruction than I had been able to take in. There was now the sound of sirens. It was actually many sirens, different kinds, coming from several directions.

The city is ours, Sammy said, and he repeated the **possessive**, each time with greater intensity: it is ours, ours, ours. He was entranced and wasn't about to notice me or complain about me to his lieutenants, but I was still making a point of not getting too close.

A police car appeared, its siren on – the first police car I had seen since all this began – and it stopped violently in front of the group, trying to cut it off. There was only one car. Where were the others? The police officer threw open his door, but by the time he had got out of his car the group had crossed the street. The police officer shouted after us in Italian, helpless and angry, and then dropped back inside his car, and chased us down, again cutting us off. Once again, the group, in the most civilised manner possible, crossed the street: well-behaved football supporters on their way back to their hotel, flames receding behind us. The policeman returned to his car and drove after us, this time accelerating dangerously, once again cutting off the group, trying, it seemed to me, to knock down one of the supporters, who had to jump out of the way and who was then grabbed by the police officer and hurled against the bonnet, held there by his throat. The police officer was very frustrated. He knew that this group was responsible for the damage he had seen driving from the ground; he knew, beyond all reasonable doubt, that the very lad whose throat was now in his grip had been personally responsible for **mayhem** of some **categorically** illegal

---

possessive: form of a pronoun (my, his, ours, etc)
mayhem: violence or chaos
categorically: absolutely, no doubt about it

kind; but the police officer had not personally seen him do it. He hadn't personally seen the group do anything. He had not seen anyone commit a crime. He saw only the results. He kept the supporter pinned there, holding him by the throat, and then in disgust he let him go.

A fire truck passed, an ambulance, and finally the police – and the police in **plenitude**. They came from two directions. And once they started arriving, they didn't stop arriving. There were vans and cars and motorcycles and **paddy wagons**. And still they came. The buildings were illuminated by their flashing blue lights. But the group of supporters from Manchester, governed by Sammy's whispered commands, simply kept moving, slipping past the cars, **dispersing** when needing to disperse, and then regrouping, turning this way, that way, crossing the street again, regrouping, reversing, with Sammy's greasy little lieutenants bringing up the rear, keeping everyone together. They were well-behaved fans of the sport of football. They were once again the law-abiding supporters they had always insisted to me that they were. And, thus, they snaked through the streets of the ancient city of Turin, making their orderly way back to their hotels, the police following behind, trying to keep up.

'We did it,' Sammy declared, as the group, now exhausted, reached the rail station. 'We took the city.'

---

plenitude: a great number
paddy wagons: police vans
dispersing: spreading out, breaking up

What the WUSA means to me

Julie Kotz Richie

Women's soccer is thriving in many parts of the world, now, and especially so in the USA, which has the largest professional league in the world. There, players attract large crowds, and the women's game has a higher profile than the men's. Whilst this is not true of all countries (certainly not the UK), the WUSA (Women's United Soccer Association) provides a good model of what can be achieved. In this article Julie Kotz Richie describes the effect of the WUSA on her life so far.

I recently watched an old videotape of my twelfth birthday party. Twenty screaming girls from my soccer team **hammed it up** for the camera, arm in arm, singing songs about soccer and shouting that our team was 'number one!' In the last scene on the video, my friend and I are lacing up our **cleats** on my front **stoop** before going to play a soccer game. Her father asks us what we want to be when we grow up. We answer simultaneously, 'We're going to be soccer players!' His response: 'No, come on. Be serious.'

My parents always insisted I could be anything I wanted to be as long as I worked hard. But, as a little girl, aspiring to be a professional athlete other than a tennis player just wasn't possible. Pele was my idol. Eighteen years later, little girls who want to be professional soccer players are not easily dismissed with a laugh. Instead, they have female role models. Mia Hamm and Brandi Chastain are

---

hammed it up: over-acted
cleats: metal hooks on top of boots to hold laces in place
stoop: porch or veranda (in USA)

now some of the most recognised athletes in the world –
male or female.

As I watched the **inaugural** game of the WUSA, I actually
cried. I cried in gratitude for these hard-working women
– for their **tenacity** in doggedly pursuing their dreams
when their fathers and society told them it wasn't
possible. Millions of little girls all over the world will
benefit from their efforts. Just as Billie Jean King was a
trailblazer for women athletes in the 1970s, Mia and
Brandi and the rest of the WUSA are now forging new
opportunities for women.

Some say that the WUSA will never make it. That
women's sports aren't exciting to watch. As a former high
school and collegiate athlete, I disagree. I played Division
One soccer for the nationally ranked Brown University
team (or more accurately, I warmed the bench). On one

inaugural: official beginning or opening
tenacity: unwillingness to give up on something, stubbornness

thrilling day during my **sophomore** year, our team played the University of North Carolina at Chapel Hill, the top-ranked team.

For once, I was glad to be standing on the bench cheering so I could marvel at the women who had dedicated their lives to soccer. The level was awesome. Mia Hamm's speed was electrifying as she ploughed through our defenders. Kristine Lilly's ball control and agility left the audience gasping. These women were serious. We lost 3–0, and we were happy not to lose by more.

I didn't have the drive or the talent to be as good as those women on the Chapel Hill team, but I am extremely thankful that they and others like them on the US National Team did. All the little girls who are passionate about soccer the way I was, now have posters of Mia and Brandi on their walls. Whereas my poster of Pele represented an **unattainable** level of soccer for women.

If I had a daughter who showed the courage, determination, courtesy and warmth toward fellow human beings that the founding members of the WUSA consistently demonstrate on and off the playing field, I would be thrilled. In an era where violence in sports routinely makes headlines, here is a group of women who are tough and muscular, yet polite and compassionate. They love what they do. They regularly sign autographs for kids, participate in soccer clinics and praise each other.

When a foul by Brandi Chastain on Mia Hamm resulted in a penalty kick that decided the first WUSA game, what did Mia Hamm do? According to Joseph White's AP story, 'After the game, I walked up to her and said sorry it had to be decided like that.' What was Chastain's reaction to

---

sophomore: second-year student at college or university
unattainable: cannot be achieved or reached

her team's loss? 'It's hard to stand up here in defeat, but it doesn't change the pride I have in my heart.' No need to say more. In an era when young girls starve themselves at eight and ten so they can look like the models on magazine covers, these kind of role models are needed.

Amy Lawrence –
football correspondent
Mike Gould

Amy Lawrence is Deputy Football Correspondent for the Sunday newspaper, *The Observer*. In this interview, she describes how she came to be a football reporter, and the skills required when reporting on a match, conducting interviews or writing features for the paper.

As a lifelong supporter of Arsenal, Amy first got into writing by submitting articles to their magazine, *The Gooner*, then after university (where she was Sports Editor for the college newspaper) she worked on *Four-four-two* magazine before moving to *The Observer.*

As football correspondent, she is generally expected to spend Saturdays reporting on a top match, and then add a couple of features during the week related to the game of football: these might be interviews with managers or players, or reflections on a football issue or incident. However, the real pressure comes on Saturdays. She tells me about the discipline of having to write an 800-word report *during* the match! Half of this has to be submitted to the editor by half-time, and then the 'top' and 'tail' of the report, at full-time. This is called the 'runner', and is usually an account of the key facts of the match, which will probably be used in first editions of the newspaper.

Then, after the press conferences, she can start to work on the second edition. 'With more time, you have a chance to be a little more creative or reflective, to assess what was important . . . if anything . . . about the game. That's where your judgement as a writer comes in, in selecting what's important, and suddenly the 800 words – which seemed so big when doing the "runner" – seem very small!'

Of course, when writing the 'runner' during the match, it's easy to miss things, and this means that amongst the journalists at the game there has evolved what Amy calls, a 'sense of togetherness', even if it is still competitive. As she says: 'You have to turn round to the guy next to you and say, "Who crossed that ball?" Nobody really minds, it's a sort of "unwritten rule" to help out.'

Has the game changed much in the time she has been reporting? She says that it has got much, much more difficult to get interviews, and get access to players. 'When I talk to older colleagues they say that it used to be quite commonplace to go to the pub after the match with players, have a chat and a drink, and it would all be quite friendly. Everybody knew where the line was drawn, but that boundary's been blurred now. There's very little trust between players, clubs and the press.' And equally important, the amount of football coverage has exploded in recent years. Now, there are specialist 32-page supplements in newspapers just on football, so the players have hundreds of requests for interviews to deal with, not just one or two.

She also cites the greater involvement of television, more magazines, radio stations and, of course, the internet – all wishing to get a piece of the football pie. And it's not easy to get 'the story'. After she and her fellow football correspondents have met on Tuesday for the weekly planning meeting, she may have to go off and contact a club or agent for access to a player or manager. 'When I first started out I had a surprising success rate, but now, basically, you brace yourself for rejection quite often.' She says that this has led to newspapers doing a greater number of profiles – that is, analysis of players, teams etc, but not necessarily with new, direct interview material. This is a different kind of skill, but is often more stimulating than actual interviews, as the latter might be with people who have nothing interesting to say!

The real pleasure of the job comes from loving football with a 'huge passion'. She recalls the first time she attended a World Cup Final, in France in '98. 'It was just a staggering experience. I remember looking at this ticket almost in awe . . . almost as if it was the secret to eternal youth or something!' Her job has allowed her to see great players and great games, and she says she often has to 'pinch herself' when she realises that she's being paid to do something she loves so much. And there is the pleasure of seeing her name in print – knowing that people are reading her words. 'Sometimes I'm on the train and I see my name on the page in someone's newspaper, and I think . . . oh my God, someone's actually reading my stuff!' Because, in the end, she says she has to write for herself. If she were to try to analyse in any real detail the huge variety of people who read her reports, it would be impossible to **cover all bases**. So she says her '. . . ground rule is to be as entertaining and informative' as she can.

As a fan first and foremost, her own favourite match has to be the game in 1989 when Arsenal beat Liverpool 2–0 at Anfield to clinch the League Championship. She was too young to report on that one, but in recent years there have been so many it's difficult to pick out one more than another. However, the very special ones are less frequent. She says there are 'games you love for the quality of the football, that make your heart sing, and there are games you love for the drama, but they don't often come together.' Nevertheless, the Juventus/Real Madrid Champions League semi-final from 2003 is memorable as one such game that had everything – drama and quality.

Of the interviews she has conducted, she says one stands out from all others, that with Sir Bobby Robson when he was manager of Portuguese side, Porto, some

---

cover all bases: make everyone happy

years ago. She recalls how he talked about the highs and lows of his job as England manager, and how he answered with 'real, genuine, alive feeling' on questions he must have been asked a thousand times – such as on the World Cup semi-final defeat to West Germany, Maradona's handball, and so on.

And finally, to the issue that will interest many – being a woman in what must often seem very much a man's world. Surprisingly, perhaps, there have been few moments when life has been made difficult for her because of her gender – indeed, to some extent being a woman has helped her stand out a little amongst the crowd of journalists. Also, she feels it might even have helped in interviewing as perhaps she is seen as less threatening than a 'hardened male **hack**'. This, added to the fact that she considers herself 'quite a good listener', has enabled her to succeed.

As for the football writers she herself admires, she mentions Paul Hayward of the *Daily Telegraph* and Patrick Barclay, of the *Sunday Telegraph,* the latter clearly a **mentor** and friend from the time she started out, learning the ropes. But, ultimately, it's clear that her own knowledge and love of football are what matters – both to readers and to people in the game. Asked whether she sees herself as a writer who views football as a stepping-stone to other things, she repeats what she said earlier, that football is her passion. 'People often think I came into this as a writer first, and that football came later. It was absolutely the other way round – so I think that tells me this is my ***métier*** – as a *football* writer.'

---

hack: a writer, often a journalist, who will write anything, providing he or she is paid

mentor: someone with experience and knowledge, who trains or advises those who are younger or less experienced

métier: speciality, activity in which you are successful

In Iraq, young players dream of Premiership glory

Alan Hubbard

Have chances of soccer stardom been improved by the overthrow of Saddam Hussein? In this article, Alan Hubbard, writing from Saudi Arabia for *The Independent* looks at the opportunities for young players in the volatile and difficult aftermath of the second Gulf War.

In Iraq, young players dream of Premiership glory

The day they buried Uday Hussein was the day Iraqi football rose again. High in the mountains of southern Saudi Arabia the nation whose players had been tortured for years by Saddam's **psychotic** son have rediscovered their pride, dignity and ability not only to win again but also to play without fear. Now they are even dreaming of playing in the English Premiership.

The appearance of Iraq in the International Friendship Tournament last weekend was their first since the fall of Saddam. Their young Olympic squad beat their

---

psychotic: having a serious mental illness, losing touch with reality

Saudi counterparts 1–0 in the opening game. The Iraqi team even has its own Michael Owen – 21-year-old Younis Mahmoud, a striker named man of the match in both of their first two games and scorer of a **hat-trick**.

Only a few hours before the first game, Uday and his younger brother Qusay had been buried in Iraq. 'It is as if a great weight has been lifted from us,' said Ali Riyah, Iraq's leading sports journalist, who was once imprisoned and tortured for a critical match report. 'No more terror in our players' eyes. No more returning home to pain and humiliation if our boys are defeated.'

It was, said Mr Riyah, not only ironic, but surely symbolic. 'Now we are free to play the game all Iraqis

love as we would wish.' Two days later Iraq defeated the leading Saudi club side 5–1 and are now favourites to win the 10-team tournament featuring national teams from Syria, Morocco, Senegal and Iran.

Uday was the self-appointed head of both the nation's football and Olympic bodies. While the current Olympic side is still too young to have been exposed to Uday's **sadistic** excesses, the senior national team did not escape the beatings on the soles of their feet, toes broken by iron bars, imprisonment and threats to cut off their legs and feed them to ravenous dogs.

Several members of the national team received such treatment for losing matches, playing poorly, or even missing penalties. So,

hat-trick: three goals by one person
sadistic: enjoying causing pain – physical or mental – to another person

too, did their former team manager Najah Hryib, who has taken over from Uday as president of the **reconstituted** Iraqi Football Federation and is here as head of their delegation. He was sent to Uday's private prison for 20 days when his team failed to win a tournament in Thailand, and although he says he was not physically tortured, his head and eyebrows were shaved as a sign of public humiliation.

Ali Riyah, now chief editor of Iraq's new sports daily *Al-Qadissiya*, fared far worse. When Uday took exception to one of his match reports, he was imprisoned, beaten and tortured with electrodes. 'Uday's cruelty knew no bounds. No one was safe from him – entertainers, sportsmen, journalists. He hated us all. He enjoyed our suffering. He never inflicted it himself, but liked to watch. He was really evil – far, far worse than his father.'

---

reconstituted: put back together from original parts

Mr Riyah now has heart problems 'and many other ailments' as a result of his treatment. Some players, too, bear mental and physical scars. After being sent off, the former national team captain Yasser Abdul Latif was sent to a prison camp, flogged with electric cable and then thrown with open wounds into a tank of raw sewage. A top referee who refused to fix a club match was also beaten unconscious and made to lie face down in sewage.

The tall, dignified Hryib, as the new face of Iraqi football, said: 'Under Uday we lost all contact with the football world. He did not allow courses for referees or coaches, no books to help us. Now we are free again and must look to the future.'

But that future is financially insecure. The reserves in the federation's account have been frozen by America, and Iraq's only major national stadium in Baghdad was destroyed by **coalition** raids.

The Iraqis know they may have to sell some of their best players to overseas clubs. Abbas Rahim has just become the first player to be signed by a Kuwaiti club from Iraq since the 1990 invasion and several of their players here have Premiership potential, notably Younis Mahmoud.

In the past, Uday pocketed half the transfer fees and tiny salaries of all Iraqi players. A good performance might have earned them a house or a car – a bad one imprisonment and a beating.

Iraq's 20-team national league is due to resume in October. 'When football is being played again regularly in Iraq it may help to bring some stability,' says Hryib.

---

coalition: alliance of groups or states sharing similar aims

Football's tycoons chase the dream

Brian Wheeler

In this article for BBC News online, Brian Wheeler looks at the rich men and women who have attempted to succeed in a business that is notorious for soaking up money. Not many have managed to come out on top, and several have seen millions lost.

The new owner of Chelsea football club, Roman Abramovich, joins a long list of business tycoons seduced by the glamour of top-level football.

A football club may be the ultimate rich person's plaything. But unlike fast cars and yachts, it gives the average billionaire something money can't buy – respect. The opportunity to play the local hero – and milk the **acclaim** of the crowd – has proved to be a powerful lure over the years. Even though, financially, the figures rarely add up.

'Profligate spending'

Chelsea's new owner does not have to look far for an example of what can go wrong. Harrods boss Mohamed Al Fayed bought Chelsea's Premiership rival and South London neighbour Fulham in a blaze of publicity, signing up a string of expensive foreign players and top manager, Jean Tigana. But the club recently announced

---

acclaim: praise, applause

record losses of £33.6 million – the second biggest in Premiership history. Reviewing Fulham's financial year, which included its first season in the top flight, in which they finished 13th and reached the FA Cup semi-final, a chastened Mr Al Fayed had a message for the fans.

'The days of **profligate** spending are over and we subsequently must tighten our belts.'

Premiership winners

Fulham's losses were topped only by those at Leeds, another club that gambled on glory and lost. The maddening thing for Mr Fayed and deposed Leeds chairman Peter Ridsdale is that it is not impossible to buy success. Just very difficult. Steel **magnate** Jack Walker pumped millions into Blackburn Rovers, transforming the sleepy first division club into Premiership winners in 1995. The reclusive millionaire shunned the limelight and never even became the club's chairman. But he is believed to have spent about £30 million on Ewood Park and lavished more than £80 million on players.

'Sad failure'

The dream eventually turned sour, with Blackburn briefly sliding back into the first division. But Walker, who died in 2000, had achieved his boyhood dream of seeing his team win the league and had few regrets. More typical is the experience of Amstrad entrepreneur Alan Sugar, who characterised his time as Tottenham Hotspur chairman as 'a sad failure'. He sold the club in 2000 for £22 million, £14 million more than he had paid for it, but success on the pitch had been thin on the ground.

---

profligate: very extravagant or wasteful
magnate: wealthy and powerful businessman

Unappealing formula

Sugar came in for criticism from some fans for not
spending enough on players. But his shrewd grasp of
finance made the salaries demanded by Premiership stars
appear absurd, with **revenue** passing straight through the
club to players, leaving little left over for profit. Sugar
memorably commented that football's finances were 'like
drinking prune juice while eating figs'. The formula may
sound an unappealing one – but there has never been any
shortage of takers. Crooked *Daily Mirror* magnate
Robert Maxwell offered the textbook example of how not
to do it. He presided over the rise and fall of Oxford
United before his death in 1991, probably saving the club
from financial ruin but alienating the fans with his
abortive plan to merge Oxford with Reading to create
Thames Valley Royals.

New idea

Maxwell then installed his son Kevin as chairman,
leaving the club £10 million in debt, switching his
allegiances to Derby, where his money and luck
eventually ran out.

Other controversial figures to have had a hand in their
local clubs include Italian prime minister Silvio
Berlusconi, whose control of AC Milan has led to
accusations of conflict of interest. Industrialist Bernard
Tapie led French side Marseille to the European Cup in
1993, before being convicted of match-rigging and fraud.

In the UK, the idea of making serious money from
football is a relatively new one. Chairmen and directors
used to regard themselves as '**custodians**' of the club.

---

revenue: money from sales
custodians: guardians or keepers

Show business

Dividends were limited by FA rules to prevent profiteering and **asset-stripping**. This all changed in the 1980s when Spurs chairman Irving Scholar worked out a way of sidestepping the rules by creating a **PLC** holding company, which could be **floated** on the stock exchange.

By the time the FA scrapped Rule 34, which limited directors' income, an influx of television money had transformed football into a branch of show business. But even as late as 1989, Martin Edwards was ready to sell Manchester United to entrepreneur Michael Knighton for £10 million. Edwards decided instead to oversee the transition of the club into a PLC, before nearly selling again – to BSkyB – for £623 million.

Dreaming on

Few clubs will emulate Manchester United's success, both on and off the pitch. But it will not stop the fans – and the chairmen – from dreaming.

---

asset-stripping: act of selling parts of a company for quick money and to make the profits look good (often temporarily)
PLC: public limited company
floated: shares of a company offered for sale on the stock market for the first time

Activities

They said what?

In reality, this is not a text at all, more like a range of fragments and snippets that have been overheard and recorded and then put into books for the readers' amusement.

1 The texts have been divided into two categories: *Metaphors and more* and *Getting your point across*.

In *Metaphors and more*, all the quotations feature managers or players trying to use more colourful language to illustrate what they want to say, and in most cases they do this by using (or misusing) metaphors.

> A metaphor is a phrase or sentence in which someone or something is described as if it were something else altogether.
>
> For example, a football team could be described in the following way:
>
> 'the **tide** of red shirts **swept** towards us in **waves**'

People associated with football often use a particular type of metaphor – *clichés*. These are phrases which have been used so much that they no longer have any real meaning, e.g. 'I'm over the moon'.

Commentators also often mix two well-known metaphors or clichés together. Who mixes up these two metaphors?

'He's put his head on the block'
'Out of the frying pan into the fire'

2 Peter Jones misuses the metaphor 'Always the bridesmaid, never the bride'. What does this metaphor mean? Why (if it had been used properly) would it have been a *good* description for Leicester?

3 Dean Holdsworth deliberately misunderstands the use of the word 'dive' in his statement. What does it mean to 'dive' in football?

Here are a number of other football words. What other meanings can they have? Use a dictionary if you need to.

net   *cross*   *dummy*   *pass*   *send off*

4 In *Getting your point across*, at least one of the quotations involves a manager contradicting himself (making a statement and then saying the opposite thing immediately). Which manager does this?

5 Write your own humorous post-match interview between a reporter and either a manager or a player. Write it as a script. In it, you should include:

- one mixed metaphor (preferably including clichés)
- one example of the person contradicting him or herself

For example:

GARTH CROOKS: So, happy with the result, Dave?

DAVE MANAGER: It's the icing on the cherry, Garth.

Darran Medley, kit designer

This is essentially an *informative* text that seeks to *explain* the job of a football kit designer. However, like many such texts, it is not wholly factual – it also features Darran's own views on particular shirts and different styles.

Nevertheless, the dominant style of the text is informative. We learn about:

- who Darran works for
- the history of the company
- how a kit is designed
- the change in styles and fashions over recent years.

1 Find and note down one thing we learn for each of the bullet points above.

For example, for the fourth bullet point we find out that it was the black kits worn by Manchester United that forced referees to start wearing green.

2 Having read this, and had your own thoughts about designing a kit, what would you consider to be the main factors a kit designer has to consider nowadays? Make a ten-point list. For example:

> Point 1: The kit has to look attractive and fashionable.
> Point 2: Choose colours such as . . .
> Point 3:
> Point 4:

Laura Green, painter of football grounds

1 This article starts with an explanation of the *neologism* (made-up word) 'groundhopper', used to describe someone who visits as many football grounds as they can. Look at the two lists of words below. Create your own neologisms by linking words from each list, and then write a definition of each new word you have created.

For example:

sun-hoarder: *someone who sits in the only remaining area of sun in a garden and refuses to give up their space!*

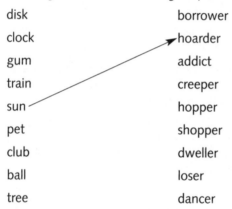

disk   borrower

clock   hoarder

gum   addict

train   creeper

sun   hopper

pet   shopper

club   dweller

ball   loser

tree   dancer

2 In explaining the work she does, Laura naturally uses linking words such as 'so' and 'because'. For example:

'**So** with my work I'm trying, consciously or sub-consciously, to bring the two [football and art] together. It forces my friends to react to art. **Because** it's about football they're automatically interested.'

Now, in your own words, write an article for a magazine. First decide what kind of magazine you will write for and who your audience will be. Briefly describe what Laura does, and then use connectives such as 'because' and 'so' to explain what is unusual.

Hating football

Andrew O'Hagan's account of how he came to hate football is organised fairly distinctly into a number of sections, each one slowly building up a picture of how a ten-year-old boy came to dislike the game his father loved. But how is this account structured?

1 Here are a number of paragraph descriptions. Read the extract again, and identify which paragraph is being described in each case.

   a School mates leave; Andrew leaves the house in a huff.
   b Mr Knocker and school-life.
   c Dad arrives in no mood for the party.
   d Party guests forced to go to another room.
   e The party begins and guests arrive.

2 The enjoyment of this extract largely comes from the amusing picture drawn by the writer. He does this by exaggerating or painting ridiculous images. Each of these has a grain of truth in them, but is made funny by O'Hagan's description. For example, he mentions the 'several rounds of pass-the-parcel without the aid of oxygen' in the tiny room his father has banished them to. Clearly, there *is* oxygen, but the statement creates a comic picture in our minds of small children all crammed unhappily into a tiny space.

Find at least three other examples of exaggerated ideas and say what has been exaggerated or invented. Here are some clues:

- *television*
- *school friends leaving the house*
- *writer's fantasy in swing-park*
- *punishment for ruining soccer shirts.*

3 This form of writing is often called creating a 'conceit' –
   putting an idea in the reader's mind for entertainment
   value. Write your own humorous account for people your
   own age to read, based on one of the following ideas:

   • a ruined holiday
   • a disastrous interview for a job
   • a first date with a boy/girl.

Among the thugs

Bill Buford uses a range of sentence structures to convey the dream-like quality of the experience, punctuated by clear images. These are often presented as simple, short sentences, using a range of types of punctuation to aid meaning.

'A shop: its door was smashed.'

He also conveys the excitement and unreality of the situation through his own contrasting thoughts:

'I felt nothing would happen to me. I felt that anything might happen to me.'

And he switches narrative perspective. On occasions, he is part of the crowd.

'We moved on.'

Later, he is outside the group, looking in, observing.

'They were well-behaved fans of the sport of football.'

1 Write your own account of someone who is with a group, but also feels outside it – perhaps because of a secret, or because they don't like or feel comfortable with the group.

For example:

- A teenager invited to a party at someone's house with older people from a different part of town.
- Someone's first day at a new job.

a Remember to switch narrative perspectives. For example:

We were all called into the manager's office. The tall secretary sneered at the manager behind his back, and the others laughed. They were enjoying themselves.

b Use some short sentences with a range of punctuation to convey images as they're seen. For example:

Someone had put a welcome gift on my desk. A cup of coffee: it was stone cold.

What the WUSA means to me

Like Andrew O'Hagan's piece, Julie Kotz Richie's account of football in the United States begins with a birthday party, but there the similarity ends. This is altogether more serious in tone and has several strong points to make. The style is different too, with no attempt to paint the humorous and exaggerated pictures that O'Hagan does.

1 How have things changed for female players in the eighteen years since Julie's twelfth birthday party? Consider:

- *the response from people to the idea of women as players*
- *the role models Julie had as a child, and those available now.*

You could start your response as follows:

As a child, despite her interest in football, Julie found it difficult because . . .

2 This text is very much about an older, wiser person looking back. She acknowledges that she didn't have the drive to become a top player, but she also recognises that top players don't have to be violent to make it.

Write an account for a football magazine from the point of view of an older, retired professional footballer, who perhaps played in the 1970s or early 1980s, looking back at his life. The account should contain the following information:

- what life was like for him as a professional in those days
- how he sees things have changed now
- his *perspective* on what his life *was* like and *is* like. Did he make mistakes? Does he wish he'd played nowadays? What would he change in his past if anything?

You may need to do some research. Look up famous players from the past such as Peter Osgood or Kevin Keegan and find out what they said about their lives then.

Amy Lawrence – football correspondent

1 The interview is organised into a number of paragraphs, each with a purpose. Here is a summary of three of the paragraphs from the interview. Find the paragraph in the text that matches each summary.

- love of football, Arsenal and first magazine she wrote for
- writing the 'runner' during the game
- her favourite interview.

2 a Look at the individual paragraphs. Did they have to be written this way? Look at the second paragraph describing the Arsenal/Liverpool match on page 149. Why can't the sentences just be switched around? Think about:

- use of connective words such as 'Nevertheless'
- tenses – 'She was too young. . .'
- the order of the information given.

b Try re-writing the paragraph so that the Juventus/Real Madrid game is mentioned first.

3 Imagine you are a football correspondent for a Sunday newspaper.

a Look through the main details of a match you are watching.

Rovers (R) vs United (Utd); Stadium: New River Lane

1st half:

3 min: Blakewood (R) yell. card – kicking the ball away; 10 min: Blakewood scores: free kick 30 yards; 30 min: Utd equalise. Penalty: taken by Stewart after foul by Skinley on Stewart himself; 32 min: R's keeper, Greene, substituted – hurt in collision with goalpost. Good game – end to end

2nd half:

Dull – no incidents, no shots on goal till 89 min.
Blakewood scores, put thru' by De Raggio. Offside.
Blakewood swears at linesman. Red card!

90 min: Utd winner. From corner, R's new keeper
Shamrazi fumbles and Stewart scores.

Final score 1–2.

b Write the 'runner' – the basic match report (200–250
words) in 20 minutes.
c Then write a second version in which you focus on
Blakewood's behaviour and ability. You can make up as
many details as you wish, but do not change the basic
facts of the match.

In Iraq, young players dream of Premiership glory

1 Look at the organisation of the first part of this article:

Paragraph	Main idea
1	Juxtaposes burial of Saddam's son, Uday, with rebirth of Iraqi football.
2	Simple report of Iraq's participation in International Friendship Tournament and the Iraqi 'Michael Owen'
3	Link back to Uday's burial, and words from journalist Ali Riyah.
4	More from Riyah, and more on the International Friendship Tournament.

This is an interesting way of starting the article. The actual facts, with more detail, are given in the second paragraph.

2 Does this mean the important news has been relegated? Not really, because it is the *juxtaposition* (placing of two things side by side) of Uday's death with the rebirth of Iraqi soccer that interests the writer. This is not just a report about the tournament. In fact, what *is* the main focus of this article?

Think about which of these seems closest to describing the article:

- Iraq's new football team's success in a tournament.
- The shadow cast by Uday over football in Iraq until his death.
- The concerns over raising money for the game in Iraq.
- The emergence of a 'Michael Owen' style player.

Football's tycoons chase the dream

This article catalogues the range of people who have owned football clubs in recent years, and their successes and failures. For each one, the writer attaches a noun, adjective or verb (acting as an adjective) in front of the person's name to give us an easy-to-remember idea of the person concerned.

For example: 'a chastened Mr Al Fayed'.

1 To whom do these other brief descriptions refer?

- 'Crooked *Daily Mirror* magnate'
- 'deposed Leeds chairman'
- 'reclusive millionaire'

This is a common feature of news articles – especially in headlines – where it is important to get news or information across in as few words as possible.

Invent a headline for each of these news stories:

- Footballer who was once an alcoholic seen checking into The Priory (clinic where people go to overcome an addiction)
- Prime Minister looks tired at his birthday celebrations.

2 Write an essay arguing either for or against the idea that you can buy success as the owner of a football club. Before you start writing, go through the article and make a note of evidence that you can/cannot buy success, using a table like the one below.

Can buy success	Can't buy success
Example of Sir Jack Walker – Blackburn Premiership champions	Same team, Blackburn Rovers relegated several seasons later

3 The Manager of the Year is often given to the person who has won the Premiership – on the basis that this is the top trophy in domestic football. Occasionally, it goes to someone else – perhaps to the manager who has done most with the limited money available, or in other difficult circumstances.

Decide your criteria for choosing Manager of the Year.

- Do they have to have won a trophy?
- Should they have developed young British players?

Comparing texts

Not surprisingly, given that they were both written by the same person and for the same website, the style and form of the two articles by Simon Inglis are very similar.

Both arise from interviews with their subjects: Darran Medley, the kit designer and Laura Green, the painter of football grounds. What other similarities can be found?

1 Here are some possible areas of comparison. Go back to the two articles, and make notes under each of these headings:

   • Opening lines (in bold) – where they are from, who is speaking
   • Length of article
   • Use of questions
   • Use of direct and indirect (or reported) speech
   • The writer of the article
   • The subject of the article (the person it is about)
   • The purpose of the article
   • The style of the article (with examples) – humorous? descriptive? analytical?
   • Your own reaction – do you find one of the articles more interesting than the other? If so, why?

   When you have finished your notes, write a *comparative* essay on the two texts, discussing their similarities and differences, and ending with a personal response to them. Make use of appropriate linking and connecting words and phrases, such as 'on the one hand', 'however'.

2 **The use of modal verbs**

   Modal verb constructions are extremely useful for all forms of writing, but particularly when you wish to explore an idea when discussing a text.

Modal verbs are verbs that add to or *modify* the meaning of a main verb. For example, in the article on Iraq, here are two sentences:

'The Iraqis know they **may** have to sell some of their best players to overseas clubs.'

'A good performance **might** have earned them a house or a car.'

In both cases, the modal verbs express *possibility* or *uncertainty*.

Other modal verbs include:

can/could   will/would   shall/should   may/might must/ought

and their negative forms such as *can't/couldn't*.

Remember, these can also be used with other auxiliary verbs such as 'be' and 'have', e.g. 'I should have been there'.

They are very useful if you want to speculate or explore an idea in an essay on a text. For example, if you were writing about a Shakespearean character, you *might* write:

Shakespeare **might** be saying that if you are too ambitious, eventually you **will** end up unhappy, or worse.

Now, imagine you have received an email from a friend, asking if you want to go with him or her to a football match or a film. Write two replies, each using a variety of modals for different purposes. In the first, you should come across as unsure about whether you want to go. In the second, you definitely *don't* want to go.

Grid matching activities to Framework objectives for KS3

The texts and activities in *Perfect Match* are progressively more challenging, moving from more accessible pieces early in the book to more demanding ones later on. For this reason, there are few Year 9 objectives for the first two sections, and few Year 7 objectives for the last two.

Text	Year 7 objectives	Year 8 objectives	Year 9 objectives
The Munich air crash	R1 Locate information R8 Infer and deduce	S4 Tense shifts	
Don't call her Ronaldinha	R4 Note-making W3 Exploratory writing		
Footballers' wives tell their tales	S15 Vary formality R9 Distinguish writer's views W1 Drafting process	S12 Degrees of formality R5 Trace developments	
The first Indian footballer	R7 Identify main ideas W3 Exploratory writing	R10 Development of key ideas	
Watching the treble	S11 Sentence variety R8 Infer and deduce, R12 Character, setting, mood	S2 Variety of sentence structure	
Corner flags and corner shops	S2 Noun phrases R8 Infer and deduce W14 Evocative description	R5 Trace developments	
Section 1: Comparing texts	R3 Compare presentation W14 Evocative description	R5 Trace developments R11 Compare treatments of same theme	
Football's history	R1 Locate information, R2 Extract information R3 Compare presentation W10 Organise texts appropriately W11 Present information		

Key
R = Reading, S = Sentence level, W = Writing, Wd = Word, S&L = Speaking and listening

Text	Year 7 objectives	Year 8 objectives	Year 9 objectives
The business of football	R3 Compare presentation R5 Evaluate sources S13 Stylistic conventions of non-fiction W11 Present information W12 Develop logic		
Football and royalty	W6 Characterisation	S12 Degrees of formality S13 Change over time	
The wonder of Ruud	R4 Note making W15 Express a view W16 Validate an argument	R6 Bias and objectivity W14 Develop an argument	
Riot in Glasgow	R8 Infer and deduce S18 Sentences in older text	R5 Trace developments S13 Change over time	
The Hillsborough disaster	R7 Identify main ideas W7 Narrative devices	Wd13 Ironic use of words R8 Transposition W7 Establish the tone	
Pupil excluded over Beckham crop	R7 Identify main ideas R8 Infer and deduce R9 Distinguish writer's views	W17 Integrate evidence	
Ronaldo and World Cup Final 2002	R14 Language choices	Wd11 Figurative vocabulary R4 Versatile reading R5 Trace developments R6 Bias and objectivity	R6 Authorial perspective Wd7 Layers of meaning
Section 2: Comparing texts	R4 Note-making R14 Language choices	R1 Combine information R5 Trace developments R11 Compare treatments of same theme	W17 Cite textual evidence
Tudor football	Wd16 Unfamiliar language W9 Link writing and reading	Wd14 Language change S13 Change over time W9 Rework in different forms	
What do they see in it?	R12 Character, setting and mood W8 Effects of language		
Three lions	S15 Vary formality S&L9 Oral text types R1 Locate information	S&L1 Evaluate own speaking	

Key
R = Reading, S = Sentence level, W = Writing, Wd = Word, S&L = Speaking and listening

Text	Year 7 objectives	Year 8 objectives	Year 9 objectives
And Smith must score		R7 Implied and explicit meanings S&L8 Conveying messages S&L16 Evaluation of performance	
The football shirt	R6 Active reading R8 Infer and deduce R12 Character, setting and mood	R5 Trace developments R7 Implied and explicit meanings	
Bend it like Beckham	R6 Active reading R8 Infer and deduce R12 Character, setting and mood	R4 Versatile reading W17 Integrate evidence	Wd7 Layers of meaning W17 Cite textual evidence
The moment of contact		Wd8 Use linguistic terms Wd11 Figurative vocabulary W5 Narrative commentary	Wd6 Terminology for analysis Wd7 Layers of meaning W5 Narrative techniques
The story of Jorge		R2 Independent research R5 Trace developments R10 Compare treatments of same theme	Wd7 Layers of meaning W17 Cite textual evidence
An evening with Gary Lineker	S&L15 Explore in role	S&L14 Dramatic techniques W3 Writing to reflect W16 Balanced analysis	W6 Creativity in non-literary texts
Arrival		R5 Trace developments R10 Development of key ideas	S&L14 Convey character and atmosphere W11 Descriptive detail
Section 3 Comparing texts		R11 Compare treatments of same theme W17 Integrate evidence	R7 Compare texts R8 Readers and texts W17 Cite textual evidence
They said what?		Wd11 Figurative vocabulary W6 Figurative language	
Darran Medley, kit designer		R10 Development of key ideas W10 Effective information	W9 Integrate information
Laura Green, painter of football grounds		Wd7 Links and meaning S6 Grouping sentences S7 Cohesion and coherence	Wd8 Connectives for developing thought

Key
R = Reading, S = Sentence level, W = Writing, Wd = Word, S&L = Speaking and listening

Text	Year 7 objectives	Year 8 objectives	Year 9 objectives
Hating football		S6 Grouping sentences S7 Cohesion and coherence W7 Establish the tone	Wd7 Layers of meaning W7 'Infotainment' W11 Descriptive detail
Among the thugs		S3 Colons and semi-colons R7 Implied and explicit meanings W5 Narrative commentary	S2 Punctuation for clarity and effect W5 Narrative techniques
What the WUSA means to me		R10 Development of key ideas R16 Cultural context W5 Narrative commentary	R6 Authorial perspective W5 Narrative techniques
Amy Lawrence – football correspondent		S4 Tense shifts Wd6 Paragraphing and cohesion W10 Effective information W12 Formal description	W7 'Infotainment' W11 Descriptive detail
In Iraq, young players dream of Premiership glory		R5 Trace developments R10 Development of key ideas W13 Present a case persuasively	R6 Authorial perspective W13 Influence audience
Football's tycoons chase the dream		W10 Effective information S9 Adapting text types	W14 Counter argument
Section 4: Comparing texts		S5 Conditionals and modal verbs R10 Development of key ideas	S4 Integrate speech, reference, quotation R7 Compare texts W17 Cite textual evidence

Key
R = Reading, S = Sentence level, W = Writing, Wd = Word, S&L = Speaking and listening

Acknowledgements

Every effort has been made to contact copyright holders of material reproduced in this book. Any omissions will be rectified in subsequent printings if notice is given to the publishers.

Extract from 'Sent Off' by Liz Jensen, from *A Book of Two Halves* edited by Nicholas Royle. Copyright © Liz Jensen. Reprinted with the kind permission of the author; Extract from *Matt Busby: Soccer at the Top, My Life in Football* by Matt Busby, published by Weidenfeld & Nicholson. Reprinted by permission of The Orion Publishing Group Ltd; 'Don't call her Ronaldinha' by Anjana Gadgil, first published on the Football Culture website. Copyright © Anjana Gadgil, 2003. Reprinted with the kind permission of the author; Extract from *Footballers' Wives Tell Their Tales* by Shelley Webb, published by Yellow Jersey Press. Reprinted by permission of The Random House Group Ltd; 'Bhaichung Bhutia' by Michael Lee, first published on the Football Culture website. Copyright © Michael Lee, 2001. Reprinted with the kind permission of the author; Extract from *Keane: The Autobiography* by Roy Keane, with Eamon Dunphy, published by Michael Joseph, 2002. Copyright © Keanepeak Ltd, 2002. Reprinted with permission of The Penguin Group Ltd; Extract from *Corner Flags and Corner Shops: The Asian Football Experience* by Sanjiev Johal, published by The Orion Publishing Group. Reprinted by permission of the publishers; Extract from *Philip's Encyclopedia 2001*. Copyright © George Philip Ltd, 2000. Reprinted with the kind permission of the publishers; Figures from 'Sport operating profit for season 2001/2002', used with the permission of the Sports Business Group at Deloitte; Extract of text and illustrations from *The Utterly Nutty History of Footy* written and illustrated by Martin Chatterton, published by Puffin, 1997. Copyright © Martin Chatterton, 1997. Reprinted with permission of The Penguin Group Ltd; 'The Vital Statistics' from *United* May 2003, Issue 128. Reprinted with the kind permission of the Editor and Manchester United Football Club; 'The Hillsborough Disaster, 14 years on' from *The Guardian*, 15th April 2003. Copyright © *The Guardian*, 2003. Reprinted with permission; 'The sparkling jewel in Brazil's world crown' by Alan Pattullo, from *The Scotsman*, 1st July 2002. Reprinted with permission of *The Scotsman*; 'What do they see in it?' by Kerry Impey, found on the Football Poets website; 'Three Lions' words and music by Ian Broudie, Frank Skinner, David Baddiel. Copyright © 1996 Chrysalis Music Ltd/Avalon Management Group Ltd. used by permission; 'And Smith Must Score' by Attila the Stockbroker. Copyright © Attila the Stockbroker. Attila the Stockbroker is Poet in Residence, matchday PA, Announcer and DJ at Brighton and Hove Albion FC. He sometimes performs poems on the pitch before home games! To access Attila's website go to www.heinemann.co.uk/hotlinks and type in express code 0870P; Extract from *United on Vacation* by Linda Hoy, published by Walker Books. Copyright © Linda Hoy, 1994. Reproduced by permission of Walker Books Ltd, London SE11 5HJ; Extract from *Bend it like Beckham* by Narinder Dhami, published by Hodder & Stoughton Ltd. Reprinted by permission of Hodder & Stoughton Ltd. Copyright © Narinder Dhami and Kintop pictures/Bend It Films/Roc Media Ltd. Extract from 'Them Belgiums' by Christopher Kenworthy, from *A Book of Two Halves* edited by Nicholas Royle, published by Phoenix, 2001. Copyright © Christopher Kenworthy. Reprinted with the kind permission of the author; 'Sobras the Sacrifice' by Simon Ings, from *A Book of Two Halves* edited by Nicholas Royle, published by Phoenix, 2001. Copyright © Simon Ings. Reprinted by permission of Mic Cheetham on behalf of the author; Extract from *An Evening With Gary Lineker*, first published by Josef Weinberger Ltd, 1992 (pka Warner/Chappell Plays Ltd). Copyright © Arthur Smith and Chris England, 1992. Reprinted by permission of Josef Weinberger Ltd; Extract from Dream Team Series VII, Episode 2 by Ben Harris. Copyright © British Sky Broadcasting Ltd 2003 and Hewland International Ltd 2003. Reprinted with the kind permission of Hewland International Ltd; 'Kit Designer, Darran Medley' and 'Painter, Laura Green' by Simon Inglis, both first published on the Football Culture website. Copyright © Simon Inglis. Reprinted with the kind permission of the author; Extract from 'Hating Football' by Andrew O'Hagan. This article first appeared in *The London Review of Books*. Reprinted with the kind permission of LRB and the author; Extract from *Among The Thugs* by Bill Buford, published by Martin Secker & Warburg. Reprinted with permission of The Random House Group Ltd; 'What the WUSA means to me' by Julie Kotz Richie; 'In Iraq, young players dream of Premiership glory' by Alan Hubbard in Abha, Saudi Arabia, from *The Independent* online, 10th August 2003. Reprinted with permission of *The Independent*; 'Football Tycoons chase the dream' by Brian Wheeler, BBC News Online business reporter, Wednesday 2nd July 2003. Reprinted with the kind permission of the BBC.